ORPHAN SLAVE SON

BEN PASLEY

Find this book online for free on many plain text, open source
book platforms. Why? Because we want everyone to read it. Find
it for sale online at every major ebook retailer in its complete
formatting thanks to www.bookshooter.com. Discover helps for
new authors at www.bookshooter.org.

Published by Blue Renaissance Publishing
Part of the Blue Renaissance Creative Group
743 Gold Hill Place, Woodland Park, CO 80866

Cover Design: Kyle Steed
Printed in the Unites States of America
ISBN: 978-0-9825434-6-7
LCCN: 2011903831

Dedicated to my wife, Robin Pasley, my best friend, who continually illuminates the beautiful truths in this book.

TABLE OF CONTENTS

PREFACE

ORPHAN

  TWO KINDS OF ORPHANS 1

    MY FIRST ON MY LIFE AS THE 6

  THE ORPHAN WORLD VIEW 10

    ORPHANS SEARCH FOR IDENTITY 11

    ORPHANS WANDER 13

    ORPHANS NEED A HOME 15

    ORPHANS STRIVE 18

  BEING A CHILD IS NOT ENOUGH 20

  ADOPTION IS THE ANSWER 23

  JESUS IS THE AGENT 28

  CHRISTIAN ORPHANS 32

    CHRISTIAN ORPHANS SEARCH FOR IDENTITY 33

    CHRISTIAN ORPHANS WANDER 37

    CHRISTIAN ORPHANS NEED A HOME 39

    CHRISTIAN ORPHANS STRIVE 41

  CHRISTIAN ORPHANAGES 44

    IS THE ORPHANAGE OUR GOOD NEWS? 45

    THE FAILURE TO THRIVE SYNDROME 49

    COMMUNITY IS A POOR REPLACEMENT 51

SLAVE

  WHO IS A SLAVE? 57

  THE SLAVE'S WORLD VIEW 58

    SLAVES WORK FOR A PLACE 59

    SLAVES COMPETE 60

SLAVES FEAR PUNISHMENT 63

SLAVES NEED DIRECTION 66

THE PARABLE OF TWO SLAVE-SONS 69

BEING SET FREE IS NOT ENOUGH 74

WE ARE SET FREE INTO FAMILY 76

ADOPTION IS THE ANSWER 79

IDENTIFYING THE DISCONNECT 81

DECIDING TO MOVE ON 83

CHRISTIAN SLAVES 86

CHRISTIAN SLAVES WORK FOR A PLACE 87

CHRISTIAN SLAVES COMPETE 90

CHRISTIAN SLAVES FEAR PUNISHMENT 94

CHRISTIAN SLAVES NEED DIRECTION 97

CHRISTIAN SLAVE TRADERS 101

SLAVERY IN MINISTRY WORK 103

SLAVERY IN DIVISIONS 107

SLAVERY IN EVANGELISM 109

SON

WHAT IS A SON? 117

RECEIVING SONSHIP 121

RECEIVE THE LOVE OF CHRIST 124

RECEIVE THE FATHER'S LOVE 130

RECEIVE THE HOLY SPIRIT 135

RECEIVE THE FAMILY 145

RECEIVE THE FATHERS 148

HOW TO SPEAK LIKE A SON 154

HOW TO PRIORITIZE LIKE A SON 158

HOW TO DREAM LIKE A SON 165

PREFACE

This is one book in a series of small books designed to help us all grow and mature as Church leaders. By *leaders* I don't mean managers or architects, I mean family influencers. The Church is a family and only leaders with family in their hearts can be expected to be helpful. I hope anyone regardless of age or experience will find this series useful in encouraging excellence in the work of loving God's people and equipping them to be who they were re-created to be. Whether you function as an apostle, prophet, pastor, teacher, or evangelist I believe this book can serve you as a leader. My hope is that anyone in leadership at any level or in any sphere of parenting influence will profit from absorbing these foundational challenges.

In the book *Tom and the Goldfish Bowl* we lifted our imaginations together to consider the differences between the kingdom of God, the Church that Jesus loves, and the traditions of men we all have to navigate. These are big themes that I consider necessary for any leader to understand. They are, in the most basic terms, explanations of what we are actually working on together and a clear understanding of them can give direction to where we are all going. In this book we will remain focused on some very large themes as well, but these will take on a more personal subject.

In this book we are going to discover the discernment tools necessary to understand how the spirit of orphanhood, the spirit of slavery, and the spirit of sonship think, act, and reveal themselves in the lives of believers. Of course it is our goal to walk as sons and to not live as orphans or slaves, but the fact remains that we are a blend of things from past and present and we need help sometimes to sort it out. Many of us are still caught walking a little or a lot under the influence of orphanhood or slavery, and it is time for us to overcome. It is time for us to mature. For those of us in leadership it is time to take responsibility in helping those we love to mature into sonship. This is my purpose in writing this book. I want to help leaders, regardless of station, learn how to discern immaturity, and how we can apply a loving touch to those in our care so we can all say with Paul in Colossians 1:28, "We proclaim him, admonishing and teaching everyone with all wisdom, so that we may present everyone perfect in Christ."

As I write I will make every effort to avoid the implication that any one human being can be categorized into a single tight little psychological category. It is not true. I hope you will forgive me if I make some mistakes in this regard as we go along. I do not wish any of us to ride the ocean of our relationships tagging people like whales—some with tags marked *orphan*, some with *slave*, others with *son*. We should not think so categorically. We are a complicated, beautiful bunch who all need room to grow. That said, each one of us would still do well to discover which of these streams of belief is flowing strong within us.

Here are a few keys to my use of language and capitalization to help you understand certain distinctions I have made in this text. Please forgive any inconsistencies. Though I like the reverent idea of capitalizing the pronouns referring to God (like *him* and *he*, for instance) I have chosen not to do it as it creates very difficult style issues. I may choose to capitalize names for ideas or things I want to assign a special emphasis—like the *Presence of God* or the *Spirit of Adoption*. Also, I always use *Church* in a formal way when I am referring to the people of God so it will always be capitalized. I will not make the error of referring to traditions of men or Church buildings synonymously with *the Church*. I may use italics to add *emphasis* (just like that), but Scripture references will be quoted according to basic literary norms and don't naturally contain italics unless I have added them.

Thank you for the privilege of sharing these thoughts with you. May God bless his beautiful Church, and may God bless your brave pursuit,

Ben Pasley

P.S. An ongoing conversation on learning to love and lead the Church can be found at www.churchthink.com.

ORPHAN

TWO KINDS OF ORPHANS

Orphaned children are a global tragedy. Global relief organizations count the figures of orphans worldwide into the tens of millions whether they are in the care of orphanages or on the streets. It is a global epidemic.

An orphan is a person who has lost connection with his parents; however, being identified as an orphan does not necessarily identify how a person has lost that connection with his parents. It could have been death or desertion. It could have been the result of war or mass displacement. Some orphans have left their parents of their own will and not under the stress of any external force, but are now lost children and can no longer find their way home. Whatever the case, the answer to the questions: *Who are your mom and dad?* or *Where are your parents?* leaves the orphaned heart with a single answer:

I don't know.

Generally, those who answer this way can be found in one of two places. An orphan may be living on his own like the tragic thousands found wandering the streets in slums, or he may be surrounded by other orphans in the care of institutions we call orphanages where they receive some kind of care. There are orphans with no houses and there are orphans who live together under a roof.

We might also make note that the orphan's age affects how we refer to them. Usually after a certain age a person is no longer referred to as an orphan regardless of whether they remain homeless or not. This is because an orphan by common definition is a child. Some orphan children grow up, integrate into society, marry, have families, and lead productive lives and eventually lose the stigma—or at least the common reference *orphan*. However, if you ask these people, even as adults, the question: *Where are your parents?,* they will answer it in the same way ...

1

I don't know.

In this book, it is not our job to understand every layer of language referring to the orphan or to unfold every part of his experience because, among other reasons, these details are beyond the knowledge of the author. We will give ourselves permission to speak in generalities because some things we can know about orphanhood are generally accepted and also generally true. We will give ourselves permission because we are human beings and as such we share many commonalities with every other version of human being on this earth.

This discussion will also provide us a map to explore how the natural tragedy of orphanhood can have an expression in our spiritual lives. In some way we could think of this as an exploration into a specific, global class of orphan: the spiritual orphan. This means there are both natural and spiritual orphans. There are many, whether living on their own in isolation or living surrounded by others in temporary religious homes, who are spiritually parent-less. There are many who walk this world who, when asked the question: *Who is your spiritual family?* or *Who is your spiritual father?* who still answer ...

I don't know.

When we hear the question, *Who is your spiritual father?* we realize that it has its own set of challenges. This question leads us to at least two distinct perspectives. The answer to that question could be taken in two directions. One could assume right away that we were referring to another human being who has acted as a spiritual guide, or a spiritual parent to whom we give the recognition *spiritual father.* On the other hand, and much larger in scope and concept, we might transcend thoughts of other people who have influenced us and jump straight to the issue of our belief in God. God, for many of us, occupies the place of being the ultimate father figure regardless of whether that position brings him honor or criticism. For many others the idea of God never takes on the reputation of a parent as he is considered to be an impersonal divine force. This kind of impersonal God would have no use for such a familial identity and would not take part in any such familial relationship. Whether we think of our answer being applied to other people or to a transcendent, fathering God the question still has legitimate weight ...

Who is your spiritual father?

This question, in my belief, has tremendous implications and our ability to answer it has tremendous consequences. The answer to this question speaks directly to who we think we are. It probably answers the basic question of human essence and personal value. It certainly speaks to us about where we came from. It defines our place in the world and our connection to other human beings. It can even project into our imaginations the future trajectory of our lives.

When a person has no satisfying answer to this question of spiritual origin, then he is truly a spiritual orphan. It doesn't matter if the disconnection with a spiritual parent was the result of death or desertion, war, or forgetfulness. It doesn't matter if orphanhood is the result of running away from others, or the intellectual denial of a spiritual world and the subsequent absence of a belief in God. It doesn't matter if a spiritual orphan lives out on the street alone, or if he lives in a great religious orphanage society full of structure and benevolent overseers. The fact remains that a person who has lost connection with his spiritual parents is a spiritual orphan, and to this point our discussion will continue.

To make sure that we are clear, I would like to affirm that I believe there are Christians, active in the Church and prominent in their religious practice, who live like orphans. I did not say they really were orphans, because if you have a heavenly Father by faith in Christ then you belong to him and he is your father. Still, there are many facts in this world that never affect the way that people live. For instance, the fact that someone is incredibly wealthy does not prohibit him from breaking into someone else's home in order to steal like a desperately poor thief. The question, you see, is not whether God knows that his children belong to him, but whether his children *know they belong to him*. There are people who have spiritually come alive to God through a relationship with Jesus, but still live as orphans because they have not come alive to his fathering love. These Christian orphans act and live without any view to their spiritual parents. I realize that for some this is difficult to hear. The very idea that there are many who love Jesus but who still live as orphans almost sounds like a philosophical—if not deeply spiritual—conflict, but I think not. It might be easier to hear if we said, "They have an orphan mindset," or "They struggle with an orphan spirit," because in these phrases we sense that we are not harshly categorizing them into actually being orphans, rather we understand they believe and live like one in opposition to their true nature.

So let's take this moment to clear the intellectual air. We are not saying that there are Christians who have not been adopted by God. We are not saying that these believers who live like orphans are not really sons in the view of the Father. What we are saying is that we know people can be adopted into the family of God, but still believe untrue things about themselves that keep them thinking and acting like orphans.

Here is an example of how this can be understood. This way of understanding the influence of the orphan-spirit in the life of one of God's sons is no different than working out the kinks in a newlywed couple's journey to overcome their old habits of being single. A newlywed couple is, by all definition, completely married even if they just entered that reality five minutes ago in a wedding ceremony. They must immediately begin to overcome *being single* in their mindset and embrace the new reality of actually being married. This way the adventure of marriage may be fully enjoyed. The challenge, however, is that a wedding ceremony which changed the legal facts for them in an instant will not change the way they think and believe automatically. The couple may be factually married in an instant, but it may take quite a while to live into the reality of marriage. So, even after they are married they might continue to think and act like single people and this, of course, robs them of the joys of marriage—not the fact of marriage. In the case of the married couple we would encourage them to take on a new mindset and a new worldview: the worldview of being joined with another person in partnership and love. We would not celebrate them when they think or act like single people in disregard for their new covenant with their spouse because this would be celebrating a reality they left behind them the day they made their vows. In the same way, our challenge in our spiritual journey is to encourage one another to see the world through our new eyes as beloved sons, and to leave behind the old eyes of orphanhood. We must work out the debilitating beliefs of orphanhood so we can fully enjoy our new lives as favored sons!

Discerning the orphan spirit that remains in each of us takes some time and we should ask the Holy Spirit to lead us. We should ask him to give us wisdom and discernment which he loves to give. We must learn to discern it so that we can see ourselves better because we are talking about a common spiritual struggle, not a rare one. We must also learn to discern this orphan influence in others so we can love the people in our care into the maturity of sonship as well.

Here is an important fact: growing older does not answer the questions of orphanhood or change the way we see ourselves. We might lose the stigma of orphanhood after years in the community of faith, but time is not the healing answer for a natural orphan or a spiritual orphan. Something specific, something great, must happen in our hearts to help us make the joyous metamophorsis into our sonship, and time just won't do it. The longer we become accustomed to our old orphan mentality and the smells of the orphanages we occupy the less we will find them unacceptable, or even unusual. The longer we remain trapped in orphanism the less our parentless situation will be a cause for concern. This book is dedicated to increasing our sensitivities to the subject and inspire us toward finding healing for our lonely, family-less hearts.

I have a friend who recently wrote a poem that tells the story of her own journey as an orphan.

MY FIRST ON MY LIFE AS THE

orphaned one,
and then,
the adopted one.
as someone's daughter I was left.
most people would say abandoned,
but she left me, so I was told,
in a place where I would be found.
i always believed that she cared.
i never thought of my father's involvement,
no one mentioned him.
i was found,
i was brought to a police station,
then,
i was brought to an orphanage.
　　　tion is foggy.
　　　tting fed,
　　　ting changed,

i was not getting touch.
the orphanage was too full,
too busy,
too much.
ever since i was born i was told that i was too much.
it started in the orphanage.
this is life:
sores,
boils,
malnourishment,
and very very sick,
nine pounds at six months.
i was told i was days from death.
my first days, weeks, were in a hospital.
i hate hospitals today,
and doctors.
i haven't been checked out in over a decade.
i cannot breathe around doctors.
i was really really hungry.
my adopted parents were scared,
and they did not know what to do,
they tried their best.
i was not fed, not cleaned, not touched,
touch was foreign.
i had learned to fight for life,
with every breath that i had,
to eat when it was offered,
to survive when i was starving.
i learned to live in the uncomfortable state of my own soil,
to breathe it in,
to not be able to escape it.
i did not even know that my needs were not being met,

i thought this was normal.
when my new parents tried to meet my needs,
receiving their help was foreign.
i did not acknowledge my needs,
because i didn't understand the importance of need,
or that there is supposed to be a response to the need,
so independence and survival was birthed.
how long did i cry?
out of hunger?
out of pain?
out of desperation?
hours ... days ... weeks ... months ...
six months to be exact.
i stopped crying.
it was not working.
i was put on a plane to america,
i met my parents in an airport,
change became normal.
people used the word *orphan,*
and then suddenly the word *daughter.*
these words are not understood.
they do not understand where the orphan has come from,
or has lived,
or has believed.
it sounds self-righteous and uncaring,
even if they are communicating the truth.
i did not come from the same world as their other daughters.
i was not treated as one,
i was part of the group.
meal times,
bath times,
sleeping beside the other orphans in our rows of beds,

we were all the same.
i was chosen to become a son or daughter,
but the choosing was created by my abandonment.
two wrongs do not make a right,
or make the right thing soothing to my heart.
a change of position,
of environment,
or even being taken care of,
does not solve the aching part of my heart that has no idea
why it is aching.
it is not about a name change,
it is not about an address.
trust was never built in my life.
i was told that I was blessed,
and that God had chosen this family for me.
in one moment i was moved from orphan to daughter.
yet the rags clung to my spirit,
and survival never left my soul.
yes, i was adopted,
i was a daughter of samuel and elizabeth moore,
but adoption didn't equal family to me,
yet.
or create a real home,
yet.
adoption took me from chaos to chaos,
then,
they took my korean name and gave me a new identity:
my name is heather bethany moore.

THE ORPHAN WORLD VIEW

For just a moment let me offer up a tender word for those who are natural orphans and may be our friends, our co-workers, or someone reading this book. Regardless of your situation if you are a natural orphan you are still a gift to this world. God planned you, made you, and has you deep in his heart. The questions and struggles you have had in this life have been both unfair and undeserved, and for that I offer my sincere sympathies. Please understand that as I speak now on the world view of the orphan I am speaking in the most general terms. I am using sweeping facts that may or may not enclose you entirely in these descriptions, and I apologize if you ever feel trapped by them. Be aware, however, I am not speaking to you as an onlooker to a world that I know nothing about. Remember, this is both a natural and a spiritual conversation. I am a human being and the realities of orphanhood find their way to me on many different planes and from many different angles in the spiritual realm. Natural orphanhood and spiritual orphanhood are both realities, and the latter has been true for all of us. This helps us understand why we all understand something about orphanhood without necessarily being natural orphans just as we can all empathize with Tiny Tim's frailty in the Dickens novel though few of us are actually crippled children. With this in mind, we can agree that both natural and spiritual orphans need adoption, and I hope you will receive this conversation as a sincere encouragement to lay hold of your sure adoption into the family of God. I pray you will read this book to the end.

Also, let's not forget this book is about three kinds of influences in our lives. These are like three ways of believing and three ways of living. We can live like orphans, we can live like slaves, or we can live as sons. We, most likely, are living as uneven blends of all three, and as we go along in this book we will see why. These three categories are natural conditions, and these three conditions are also spiritual conditions. We will take the time to define each of these conditions using natural terms because this is the easiest way to understand each, and then we will use each natural definition to help us discover what it means to our spiritual journey.

Orphans, regardless of circumstance, share a common world view and a common way of seeing themselves.

ORPHANS SEARCH FOR IDENTITY

Deep in the human soul is an instinctive need to understand the question of origin. We have an unrelenting heart-quest to understand where we have come from. It is an instinctive human need that is stuck somewhere permanently in our spiritual DNA. Overlooking this *heart-quest* is the fundamental mistake that strict evolutionists make when they stake a claim in a theory that provides no real answer to the deeper questions of origin. In evolutionary theory there is no romantic source to our beginnings, no description of the beautiful hands clapping together to create the big bang, no dreaming intellect behind the infinitely perfect clockwork of our universe ... what a tragedy! Humanity is full of romance and an origin story that is less than a dramatic love story of purpose and design is beneath us. We have deep instincts to discover the meaningful, colorful origins of our lives and our loves. The backslapping, self-congratulating, heartless, smug intellectualism surrounding this proposition of a romance-less human origin should send all of us running to Christianity as the only reasonable protest. Christianity explodes with stories of purposeful creation, a loving God, and a human family full of destiny and adventure.

The very effort evolutionists have made in reducing our human origins to a million year march from primordial ooze to well-dressed computer programmer has left us all with a gnawing dissatisfaction in their answers because they completely disregard the deeper questions, the more important questions. This is why not one decent love story can be constructed from their version. Not one life changing moral can be derived from it. Not one wholesome narrative can arise from it. This should educate the educated on how truly backward they have become. Evolution ultimately fails in the hearts—not the minds—of humanity because it does not contain the kind of romance we need to justify the tremendous sense of personal value and future worth that we instinctively know are ours. This is a global instinct, and its incredible universalism triumphs all elite think-tanks. For this reason alone we should dismiss Darwin's weak philosophy on God and man, and take up any new theories that give us better answers to our excellent questions of origin.

The question of origin is absolutely essential to our sense of self-knowing, and it is absolutely essential to firming up our sense of worth and future in this world. In real life, in the movies, and in books and literature the most well recognized plot element when an orphan is included in the script is his search for origin. There is a deep need for the orphan to find his biological parents. This could be a fictional generalization, but generalizations are there to show that something is generally true. *Generally*, orphans suffer a gnawing desire to find their biological parents.

Why the search?

The deep desire of the human soul to understand the question of origin is classically illustrated in the life of the orphan. In the way orphanhood in the natural is a living allegory for the rest of humanity in the spiritual. On a broad, spiritual plane we all suffer from the same gnawing desire: we must know where we came from. We want to know our spiritual origins. And, to raise the stakes, I believe it is more than that because the question of *who we are* can never be answered by outlining the elemental facts of *what we are*. We must also know *who we came from*.

The personal question "Who am I?" is infinitely more appropriate for the needs of our hearts because it is infinitely more romantic than the question, "What am I?" The real question in the human psyche has always been related to the *who*, not the *what*.

In the life of the biological orphan this is classically true.

In the life of the spiritual orphan this is absolutely true.

We must all answer the question "Who am I?" regardless of the cost because it is worth everything to all of us.

ORPHANS WANDER

Folklore is a creative expression, usually literary in form, that embodies the common beliefs of a culture. This creative expression often contains bits of moral teaching, or even religious insights. Orphan narratives are often found in folklore from around the world because the orphan's plight embodies cosmic challenges that we all share.

First, in folklore, orphans represent tragedy, and tragedy is a common human experience. To be isolated from even the most basic form of social structure—the family—is a great tragedy, and tragedies are where we experience deep emotion and learn about ourselves. This is the stuff of folklore.

Secondly, we all love heroes, and this sets the stage for more orphan stories in our folklore. Orphans represent the neediest of undefended souls. They call to us to defend them, and those who help the orphan are the greatest kinds of heroes. Those who will not help the orphan are the lowest form of villain. To bring harm to the orphan strikes so deep into our internal morality that we can barely even imagine it, and when we do imagine it we are immediately ready to take up weapons in their defense.

Christianity is the welcome home for this kind of chivalry. In the letter the Apostle James wrote to the Church he says, "Religion that God our Father accepts as pure and faultless is this: to look after orphans and widows in their distress" (James 1:27).

Thirdly, in folklore, overcoming adversity is a common theme. The orphan who rises above circumstance and overcomes adversity is a sign of hope for all humanity, and once again is central to this folkloric narrative. This is how we have come to refer to the overcoming underdog as a *Cinderella Story*. Cinderella was an orphan who against all odds overcame her lack of family (even while surrounded by the form of family.) Cinderella reminds us that when an orphan succeeds in life we can say to ourselves, "If they can overcome adversity and rise above, then there is hope for all of us!"

Finally, in folklore, we have stories of being lost and looking for home. Remember, folklore is simply the stories and myths a culture develops to try and answer the questions that are most important to them. The fact that finding a home is so central to folklore is a clue to how close it is to our hearts. In folklore orphans represent this *looking for home*. Orphans wander looking for home. This wandering is sponsored by the orphaned soul's need to discover the answer to questions we have already posed, and these questions are deeply engrained in the global human experience:

Who am I?
Where do I belong?
Where is my family?
Who will defend me?
Where will I rise above and find my success?
Where is my home?

All of this searching can be rudely summarized into the *need to find a place in a family*. Someone born into a family where there is basic love and belonging will find no need to look for *another place*. Location inside of a family provides the direction needed on the human compass. The family member hears the question, *Where am I on the great map of human existence?* and the answer comes, *I am right here ... here in this family.* Sonship represents fixed coordinates on our spiritual GPS, but the orphaned heart can't find its location. Without this basic sense of relational location the orphan wanders in search of it.

When we say an orphan wanders we don't necessarily reduce that to physical travel alone. We also know this means a wandering in the heart and mind. Wandering is in many ways a kind of aimless travel. The orphan travels toward the place he needs but cannot find. The orphan wanders to find the answer to the internal question: *Where do I belong?* In this way, being an orphan is a state of lost-ness, and the prospects of being found are not always in plain view. J.R.R. Tolkien said, "Not all those who wander are lost," but I say, "All who are lost will wander."

The orphan, in his wandering soul, may look for a place in many ways. Places might include an ethnic or national placement. It might include a job or career security. It might involve a kind of personal notoriety that evolves into a place in the eyes of others. A place, you see, must be found even if it is only temporary, and even if it is an incomplete answer. We know the actual place that is always needed in the life of the orphan has, and always will be, *inside of family.*

ORPHANS NEED A HOME

Let's play a basic word association game.

I say the word *orphan*.

What is the first word that came to your mind?

For many it is the word *orphanage*. This is not to say that every orphan has lived in an orphanage or that an orphanage is their only path through childhood. What it does say is that the orphanage classically defines the general plight of the orphan in our minds.

The very state of being parentless as a child demands that some kind of nurturing care be given by others. In cities around the world we find many orphans, and in poverty stricken areas we find many, many more. All orphans need care and it is in our moral instinct to give it. This call to care for the orphan gives immediate rise in every culture for the creation of the orphanage as a way to provide basic care for the many.

The orphanage provides shelter, food, and clothing. The orphanage seeks to provide some form of human care and touch. It may also provide some kind of training for life after the child grows up and and is too old to remain in the orphanage. However, though it may be filled with care-givers of every kind, the orphanage is missing what is desired the most in the heart of the orphan—parents.

In an orphanage the care that is given is absolutely necessary and it is to be celebrated. Caregivers in orphanages are to be commended as the highest stock among human kind. That being said, they are still not parents. No matter what is said of the individual caregiver's honor and decency, whenever a group of children are placed in the care of a few the tools of management must be employed, and *management* is a wholly different system than the personal, loving touch of parenting.

Management is an inescapable reality in the life of an orphanage. There are many children so mechanisms must be put in place to provide order. Schedules must be set. Mealtimes are set for all. Bath times, bedtimes, school times, and play times must be arranged in a managed rhythm for all the children. This rhythm must be adhered to if there is to be any order—if there is to be any peace—in the orphanage. Consequences and rewards must be firmly established in order to incentivize order. These schedules, rhythms, requirements, and incentives are all the tools of management, and when those who are not parents apply them then only the fruit of being managed will grow. Management may be necessary, after all, can you imagine an orphanage with no management? It would be chaos.

Many religious structures have been created whose fundamental value has been to provide orphanage care for those who have been wandering. Church, to be specific, often identifies a place for the lost to be found and to find a place. In that last sentence we can note the common words *lost, found,* and *place.* These are common words for Christians. Some Christians might as well say, "I don't know who my spiritual family is, but when I come here to these meetings I receive care, basic shelter, and someone is bringing management to the chaos of my life." Because finding a place is so basic to overcoming feeling lost many orphaned hearts are very comfortable identifying the Church as nothing more than a place, a building, or a meeting.

For many this is enough.

For many the institution of religion itself is enough to calm the chaos of orphan feelings.

For many the institutions of the Church are, indeed, welcome orphanages.

However, a building is not a home, nor an orphanage a true family.

For many the orphanage style care found in Church buildings and religious settings has been enough to partially satisfy the deeper desire to reconnect with true spiritual family. This answer, however, just like partial answers for the wandering natural orphan, can only be a temporary answer and it will not provide what the spiritual orphan really needs.

ORPHANS STRIVE

I had a friend who commented on the general facts related to the orphan spirit and he said, flatly, "Orphans steal."

"What?" I asked with some surprise.

"Orphans steal because they don't know that anything is really theirs."

This conversation was particularly difficult because there was a natural orphan in the room who took offense to that generalization for obvious reasons.

With respect, however, he went on to explain that in the orphanages he had visited in a particular overseas location one of the biggest problems was theft. Orphans were stealing anything they could get their hands on whether it was from one another, or from visitors, or from people in the villages when they were out and about. Obviously, not every orphan steals from others, but there is something to be learned from the general insight: *Orphans don't know that anything is really theirs.*

In a family there is a shared sense of ownership that is basic and assumed. Not only is there a shared sense of ownership and expectation of basic provisions like food, shelter, and clothing, there is also a future promise called an inheritance that belongs to the sons. The present and future provisions inside of family are a basic, ground floor fact, and this affects the rest of every family member's outlook on life.

The orphan, on the other hand, lives with no such basic assurance. What has been given to the orphan in an orphanage, for instance, has been given to all the other orphans with equal commitment and it is not at all permanent. Food, shelter, and clothing are part of a caring system, but not part of a personal, long-term commitment. At a certain age those provisions will be removed from the orphan. If the orphan cannot conform to the orphanage rules these provisions might also be removed.

Therefore, when it comes to personal ownership the orphan feels the need to take and defend what they can personally take and hold on to because it is not permanently guaranteed by his family. Listen to Jesus when he echoes this truth referring to slaves: "Now a slave has no permanent place in the family, but a son belongs to it forever" (John 8:35). Pardon my jump to the topic of spiritual slaves as Jesus refers to them here, but this does apply to orphans because the issues of the orphan and the slave are intertwined. The lack of family affects them both. The orphan's troubled relationship to provision is connected with a slave's troubles, and later in this book we will see why.

This is a heart lesson that can be applied to physical property, emotional property, relational property, and spiritual property. The orphan spirit has no family-given deed to any of these kinds of properties, and must work and strive to gain them. This is partly the reason why the fable of the orphan gaining success in the world appeals to our desire to overcome against all obstacles and, in effect, rise from *having nothing* to *having something* based on our own efforts. This is the journey of our own orphan-dreams and the result it this:

What we earn we will have to defend.

Spiritual orphans must defend any ground of success, place, or provision they have attained. They must defend against other orphans. They must defend against anyone who might lay legitimate claim to what they have worked to own. They might need to take whatever they can get. These are very important views into the heart of the spiritual orphan as well.

Now we have touched four general insights into the orphan spirit: orphans search for identity, orphans wander, orphans need a home, and orphans strive. All four of these issues deserve to be solved. The orphan heart needs a real, tangible rescue. We are now going to see God's own commitment to rescuing the orphan.

BEING A CHILD IS NOT ENOUGH

The God of the Bible is deeply committed to the specific issue of rescuing orphans. This rescue is not a side item or a sub-plot. His plan is so specific and so focused when we read the Bible that we might believe the whole of his work in human history is to provide a rescue from this one singular tragedy: orphanhood. We might add here, there is no other world religion or spiritual path that answers the human question of orphanhood as perfectly as the story of God's love in the Bible, and no other mythology that makes it the central theme from beginning to end like the Christian narrative. Let's discover a few basic facts that are clear in the Bible about the way God relates to this global question of orphanhood.

First, we find God's moral outrage against the abandonment of children. In the second book of the Bible , Exodus 22:22-24a, God begins to share his specific laws for human conduct. He says, "Do not take advantage of a widow or an orphan. If you do and they cry out to me, I will certainly hear their cry. My anger will be aroused, and I will kill you with the sword." Well. That was clear. For the God of the Bible the mistreatment of the orphan is a capital offense, and the punishment was not humane. This is important because it helps us understand that the heart of God rejects the situation where a person is without family connections, and God rages against those who might cause it to happen or take advantage of those who suffer from it. This moral outrage should underline something very important to all of us searching for our spiritual answers: God is committed to rescue us from orphanhood.

Secondly, in the Bible we find that *being a child of God is not enough to overcome spiritual orphanhood.* This is an unpopular but critical fact. In a very basic way we are all children of God in that we have all come from him. He made us so we can all say, "We are his children." In this use of the word, however, we can make no evaluation on the quality of relationship between the Creator and the created one. *Child* can mean something as basic as "produce." This is an insufficient state of being for us. We know we are more than produce. Paul noted this insufficiency to the Greeks in Athens, "As some of your own poets have said, 'We are his offspring.' Therefore since we are God's offspring, we should not think that the divine being is like gold or silver or stone—an image made by man's design and skill" (Acts 17:28-29). Paul's comment is just a basic stepping stone for understanding why God is not a stone or a tree, but it certainly was not a promotion for the we-are-just-his-offspring-Gospel. Paul went on to explain the love of God and unfold the work of Jesus to them because being an *offspring* was not an acceptable relationship with God for the Greeks, nor is it sufficient for us today.

It is so sad that in the mind of many philosophers a human being is simply an emanation from the will of God. This kind of thinking covers mistakes all the way from Jewish mysticism in the Kaballah to modern spiritualists and New Agers. It filled the minds of pagan intellectuals in Athens in Acts 17 who considered every man one of God's *offspring*. These same thinkers then propose that because we are all God's children that we all have an inherent eternal equality in our relationship with him. That is to say that our spiritual ground and spiritual position are equally sure. This *equal ground* idea is very popular. This assertion is the hot property of modern universalists and university educated

Christians because it spreads a wide blanket of approval from God over everyone on the earth under the lone, albeit generic, identification *child*. These folks would say that if we are God's children then we belong to God and we need to look no further for our eternal trajectory. I challenge you to reject this thinking on one basic fact alone:

Orphans are children, too.

Please answer this question, "Is every orphan a child of someone?"

The answer is, of course, *yes*.

Now answer this question, "Does an orphan child know its parents?"

The answer is *no*.

This is the crux of the matter, and this is the heart of God in the Bible. We don't want to know that we have a God somewhere —we want to know that God is our Father and that he is available to us right now! We want to know that we are his in specific, romantic, eternally familial terms.

The great human question is not, "Do I have an origin somewhere in general?" It is definitely not, "Am I a child of the cosmic emanator?" The great human question is in stark contrast to such a broad and impersonal question. It is much more specific:

"Who is my father, where did I come from, and to whom do I belong?"

The Bible considers a lack of answers to this line of questions to be morally outrageous, and universally unacceptable. In the Bible we find out that God is out to end this tragedy and he will do so in dramatic fashion. The great news for our hearts is that God is not just about the work of convincing us to overcome atheism and believe, generally, that he is real. That is not Christianity. We are not guided in the Scriptures to simply

22

overcome secularism or materialism. We are on a path to something dramatically greater. We are on a much more specific path than attaining a general agreement that we are the generic children of a generic god who has a generic plan.

We were destined for much, much more.

God wants to rescue and help every single person who has suffered disconnect from his true destiny, and deliver every single orphan from loneliness and loss into a permanent place in a *real spiritual family*. He will bring us to a place of knowing our specific relationship with him and with his own family. He will wage war on the enemies of our soul by rescuing us from our loss of family and, so, our loss of place in the universe by transporting us directly into his own family!

So what is God's *method* of rescue?

The God that we meet in the Bible is wholly and completely committed to answering the question of our origin in dramatic fashion. He will address our need for family in a specific narrative. He will conquer our orphanhood through a singular, central act.

It is the only method prescribed in the natural realm that can come close to answering the burning questions in the heart of the orphan.

It is the only reasonable answer we should all expect from a God who really understands our condition and the deepest cries of our hearts.

It is the method of *adoption*.

ADOPTION IS THE ANSWER

If this is your first deep look into what it means to follow Jesus and be a Christian then fasten your seat belts because this is very exciting!

When Jesus arrives we discover in living form exactly what we had been hoping to believe about God. Would it surprise anyone reading this book that we are going to discover the God of the Bible, now, as ...

Abba!

Papa!

Daddy!

Father!

We discover that God is, indeed, more than just God. God is a Father who is obsessed with reconnecting his family.

God, even in the Old Testament, was filled with the desire to build a two-way relationship of love with a people that he could call his own. In Jeremiah 29:11 God speaks to his people as he called them out of wartime exile and says, "'For I know the plans I have for you,' declares the LORD, 'plans to prosper you and not to harm you, plans to give you hope and a future.'" This is the kind of God we have longed for—one who is deeply invested in our value and future.

The ancient songwriter and king, David, writes of God in Psalm 39, "I praise you because I am fearfully and wonderfully made [...] My frame was not hidden from you when I was made in the secret place. When I was woven together in the depths of the earth, your eyes saw my unformed body. All the days ordained for me were written in your book before one of them came to be." This is exactly the kind of God we need. We occupy his dreams. He is a God who imagined us into being, has not lost sight of us, and has thought of us as wonderful, purposeful, and full of future. This God will not be satisfied with a generic relationship to those he created. No, he wants to create a family connection.

Look, however, in Deuteronomy 32:5 as the writer tragically states, "They have acted corruptly toward him; to their shame *they are no longer his children*, but a warped and crooked generation."

In the Old Testament we find that not all peoples of the earth were called God's children because he had chosen, like it or not, to place his family lineage, will, and identity into the sons of Abraham, uniquely. This is where the modern Jewish people find their sense of belonging in God's design, but being a son of Abraham is still not the answer we need. God was looking for a reciprocal, loving relationship with a specific people—per person —then, and he is still looking for it now. He will not be satisfied with a people who can trace a lineage to Abraham, but are not able to trace their own personal connection to God as their father. You see, God wanted people to whom he could say, "You are my sons," and the people could say in return, "We love you, Dad!"

The hard thing about discovering healthy spiritual family in the Old Testament is that people constantly failed in their attempts to reciprocate the kind of love and obedience that would identify them as sons. Jesus explained this later to the professionally religious Jews who thought their bloodline claim to Abraham was enough. He puts this to the Pharisees in John 8 when they argued:

> "Abraham is our father."
>
> "If you were Abraham's children," said Jesus, "'then you would do the things Abraham did."
>
> "We are not illegitimate children," they protested. "The only Father we have is God himself."
>
> Jesus said to them, "If God were your Father, you would love me, for I came from God and now am here. I have not come on my own; but he sent me. Why is my language not clear to you? Because you are unable to hear what I say. You belong to your father, the devil, and you want to carry out your father's desire." (John 8:39-44a)

These people were clinging to a generic definition of *child* and had no real connection to the Father themselves. They were certainly God's children, but they didn't know their heavenly Father because if they did, Jesus said, they would have recognized him as his Father's Son. To be restored to God we need more than a Jewish bloodline or a claim to divine childhood. We need a heart-level transformation so we can see God as our Father. We needed a solution that not only granted us a covenant connection with God as our Father, but would transform our internal DNA code so we could really connect with him as sons, not just as orphans renting space in his care. We needed a new heart that could genuinely cry out, "Dad, my Dad!"

This would take a miracle.

When we meet Jesus we are meeting the miracle. Jesus introduces Himself as God's son, an ambassador of family love who voluntarily came to offer the gift of restoration back into the family of God and to put into us a new life! This is why Jesus said, "If God were your Father, you would love me." God's people will love his son, Jesus.

Yes.

We hear Jesus speaking in John 3:16 one of the most well known passages in the whole Bible, "For God so loved the world that he gave his one and only Son, that whoever believes in him shall not perish but have eternal life." Jesus reveals his purpose so clearly and in this one passage he focuses it on all of us. There is no mystery in his point, or hidden meaning in his life. Jesus reveals the love of Father God for his own son, and then he reveals that this love was not for him alone, but is also for us to share!

I told you this was amazing.

It is so wonderful to meet a God who in his own nature is family. He is Father, Son and Holy Spirit. He is a loving relational

Trinity that is filled with honor, commitment, and joy for one another. It is even more amazing when we discover that his heart toward us is family as well! I told you it was going to be amazing. God's love is just the kind of love we need as spiritual orphans. God's love is a rescuing and restoring kind of love. God's love restores us into his own family not just as generic children, but as beloved sons.

You have heard people speak of the Gospel, or the Gospels? You have heard of the Good News of the Gospel? Well, here it is in a nutshell: In a letter to Christ-followers in the ancient city of Ephesus, Paul writes, "But now in Christ Jesus you who once were far away have been brought near through the blood of Christ" (Ephesians 2:13). The Good News is that we can come home and be near to God again! Jesus has done something so miraculous that it has made a way for us to return to the family of Father God!

This miraculous way is *the way of adoption.*

Jesus did not introduce Himself as God's teacher. Nor did he claim to be God's prophet. He was not pushing a new governorship, cultural improvement, social reform, or book of doctrine. He introduced himself as the son of God and he preached the kingdom of God—a kingdom of family. When he began his public work he was baptized by John in the River Jordan and when he came up out of the waters people heard this voice from heaven booming, "This is my Son, whom I love; with him I am well pleased." The very beginnings of Jesus' life and work began with the Father's love being poured out on him. The inauguration of the kingdom of God that we are invited to enter began with this same proclamation of love from a heavenly Father to his beloved Son.

Jesus goes on and shows us that he is both willing and able to share his beloved sonship with us.

JESUS IS THE AGENT

An agent is the person capable of action. *Agency* is action performed on another's behalf. Well, Jesus was the only one capable of acting on our behalf in a way that would provide for us what we really needed: *adoption!*

The best way to describe the end result of adoption is to say that Jesus has chosen to *share* his position of favored sonship with us. Romans chapter 8 is like a multi-vitamin for the soul that has returned to God. We can read it over and over again and will always be nourished. In verse 17 Paul writes, "Now if we are children, then we are heirs—heirs of God and co-heirs with Christ, if indeed we share in his sufferings in order that we may also share in his glory." Paul is not identifying us as generic children here. No. He is underlining a privilege that only the sons share—the family inheritance. He repeats this amazing promise of inheritance in his letter to the Colossian believers. In chapter 1 verse 12 he says, "Giving thanks to the Father, who has qualified you to share in the inheritance of the saints in the kingdom of light." While these verses may speak of a future inheritance, it also firmly plants us into a present reality: *We can be sons of God through our shared relationship with Christ.*

How do we share sonship with Christ?

It is through his blood.

I know that may sound harsh, and some have even said barbaric, but it shouldn't. We know that all family is a blood relationship. That is common language, and we don't consider that to be barbaric at all. We share our DNA, our personal blueprint with our children, through our bloodline. According to the Bible, though we were all loved as God's children we had broken our bloodline connection with him through our own rebellion. We had effectively left home to try and start family without him, and much too late we realized that we had been duped by evil influences and faulty logic. Our minds had failed us. Our desires had deceived us. It was all futile.

Now this is why in Biblical language we say that blood had to be applied to the situation in a new way. This is why there are so many images of sacrifice and blood in the Bible as a whole. What we are saying is that we needed a kind of transfusion with the bloodline of God because we had disconnected from the source. Blood is how family is transmitted.

God's way of establishing a new connection, a kind of transfusion of his bloodline as it were, was the way of supernatural adoption. This was to be a permanent kind of adoption that would be written not just on paper with pens that men had made, but it would be written right onto our souls and signed in the blood of Christ, his true beloved son.

I must speak to this briefly because this is a short book. There are many beautiful things to be discovered about how Christ offered his own blood in order to make a way for us to be forgiven of all our sins and rebellion and come back to God, but for now I just want to point to this one incredible passage in the Gospel of John, chapter 14. Here Jesus is speaking tenderly to his followers (I excerpt for brevity):

> Do not let your hearts be troubled. Trust in God; trust also in me. In my Father's house are many rooms; if it were not so, I would have told you. I am going there to prepare a place for you. And if I go and prepare a place for you, I will come back and take you to be with me that you also may be where I am. You know the way to the place where I am going. (John 14:1-4)

There is no reason to believe, from everything we know of Jesus and his message of the kingdom, that he was suddenly turning his attention to building a heavenly hotel. Of course he is saying there is an eternal *place* for us with God. Jesus said clearly he would come back and take them to the place he had prepared, but why do we assume this is a future place that has a room number on our door? Is that really what we have been longing for?

We have already said that the place the orphan needs most is to simply have a place of sonship in the heart of real parents. In the case of spiritual orphans we need to know that we have a place in the Father's heart. Jesus was, indeed, preparing a place of family sonship for his disciples. He was making that place available to us. The favor of sonship, and the privilege of sonship was coming available to his disciples. He was preparing that place for you and I as well. Now we can say that we know that the Father's heart has plenty of room for his kids to come home to. Father has a place in his heart for you.

Do you want to come home? Well, Thomas asked the question of home and Jesus gave him a new answer:

> Thomas said to him, "Lord, we don't know where you are going, so how can we know the way?"
>
> Jesus answered, "I am the way and the truth and the life. No one comes to the Father except through me. If you really knew me, you would know my Father as well. From now on, you do know him and have seen him."
>
> Philip said, "Lord, show us the Father and that will be enough for us."
>
> Jesus answered: "Don't you know me, Philip, even after I have been among you such a long time? Anyone who has seen me has seen the Father. How can you say, 'Show us the Father'? Don't you believe that I am in the Father, and that the Father is in me?" (John 14:5-10a)

Jesus was the son of God in every way. This is how we learn to believe in the Trinity—God is in Three Persons. I don't understand it intellectually, but if we have seen Jesus, according to his own words, we have seen the Father. The two are One-God in this way. Jesus states so clearly that he is the only way to return to the Father's heart. Only he could do it through sharing his position in the heart of his own Father as his beloved son. He was personally going to make this way. Jesus was the agent of adoption.

This way back to God would require him to die on a cross to make a way for forgiveness and restoration, but the whole point of the dying was not just to offer forgiveness and then leave us all alone. Listen as Jesus continues to speak to his disciples ...

> If you love me, you will obey what I command. And I will ask the Father, and he will give you another Counselor to be with you forever—the Spirit of truth. The world cannot accept him, because it neither sees him nor knows him. But you know him, for he lives with you and will be in you. I will not leave you as orphans ... " (John 14:15-18a)

Jesus said it very clearly, *"I will not leave you as orphans."* Orphanhood is the problem Jesus was promising to solve. It was the crisis that he was sent to repair. Now, he offers his solution. Incredible. Jesus did not promise to arbitrarily save us and then leave us alone to figure out the rest of it on our own. Jesus promised to solve the deep question of our lonely, isolated souls. The question plaguing every orphan, "Who am I?" is going to be answered by Jesus alone and proven by a unique gift that only he could make way for. He was going to ask the Father ... and then the Father was going to send us a love gift. The Father is going to send the Third Person of the Trinity—the Holy Spirit—to be with us personally and permanently.

This was Christ's way of saying, *I will come to you. I will not leave you alone.*

Have you ever heard any news that was better than that? This really is Good News! Father God loves us. His own Son has chosen to share his position of favor with us. And now, the Holy Spirit, who is the very Presence of God, has been given to us to live in us and beside us as we go. The Holy Spirit will convince us of our sonship and prove his loving favor toward us as sons is never-ending. This news is so good and so real that it has been changing millions of lives for centuries when they hear it, and believe it, and walk in it.

Do you want to walk in it?

God's plan for us all along was adoption, because God knew all along that we were—every one of us—orphans who needed a Dad. This is what it really means to become a Christian. This is how we know that the God of Christianity is the only God who has been big enough to really save us, worthy of our need for heavenly romance, and true enough to answer humanity's deepest heart cry in a satisfying way.

Friends, it is time to follow Christ and receive the beloved sonship that he is willing and able to share.

CHRISTIAN ORPHANS

Yes, I had a wonderful time in that last section of this little book just outlining the beauty of the adopting message of Christ. It is good news for every orphaned heart. I couldn't help but think of all the readers who might read those words for the very first time. I have not forgotten, however, that this book is for believers who have been called to lead the family of God and learn to love the

Church better. I took the time to underline the adoption focus of God's heart in the last section on purpose. We need to clarify our minds and consider the challenges that confront us.

As we have already said, there are Christians who still act like orphans. Some act this way a little, some act this way a lot. The reason is simple: they have not left the old ways behind. When we come to God and we are restored to family as his sons there is not an ounce in us that is really an orphan any longer. Yet, our lives are full of the habits of orphanhood and our history is full of practice. It takes time, but more than that it takes the truth of our sonship taking root in our souls and growing up into maturity to see some of these orphan-instincts lose their grip and eventually fade away. It is a kind of displacement, really. As the beauty of the truth is embraced and realized it will expand and literally force all the untruth and lies about who we really are right out of our lives.

As leaders we must become adept at recognizing the residual influences of orphanhood in our own lives first, and then in the lives of others as well. We have been called, according to Ephesians 4, "to prepare God's people for works of service, so that the body of Christ may be built up until we all reach unity in the faith and in the knowledge of the Son of God and become mature, attaining to the whole measure of the fullness of Christ." Part of this building up of others is building up their sonship so that orphanhood will be displaced.

Let's reflect on the four orphan world-views we noted in the previous section where we were speaking of orphans in the natural, and use those insights to give us tools of discernment and tips on how to begin the process of healing.

CHRISTIAN ORPHANS SEARCH FOR IDENTITY

One of the first symptoms of orphanhood in the life of a believer is the constant feeling of being lost. It is a kind of lostness that never feels quite at home anywhere and is always on the lookout for the next relationship or project to arrive and give the heart a place to rest. This kind of lostness stems directly from failing to fully answer the question, "Who am I?" and finds that inside of that failure an unrelenting lostness sets in.

Lostness in the life of the Christian orphan only comes from one thing—not knowing how much Father God really loves us, and then not being able to receive that love. It sounds so simple, but it is so true. It is more common than we think.

I recently held a small retreat for a group of young believers who had been meeting together in their homes for years as their expression of being the people of God together. Many were covered in tattoos and signs of an alternative life, but they were also covered in a great passion for Jesus and had chosen, in a way, to express their rebellion against the world by a radical kind of commitment to one another. They were, however, continuing to live as outcasts in many ways, never allowing themselves to build relationships outside of their small alternative circle. We sat down for the first meeting and someone requested, "Tell us more about the Holy Spirit."

Operating in the simplest kind of discernment related to seeing the orphan spirit on this group, I said, "I will do just that, but before I get into that let me ask you something: Do you know how much Daddy God loves you?"

I followed that question and answer time with some simple encouragements on the great love of the Father and then, suddenly, an outpouring of confession and repentance began to take place. The revelations of the Father's love started to flow. We read the story of the *Two Boys Who Didn't Know How Much Daddy Loved Them* from Luke 11. After agreeing to receive the love of the Father in a greater measure, they found out receiving the Holy Spirit was much easier.

Let me now share what the most salient feature of this group had been for all the years they were together. It was their proclamation that *we just don't quite belong. We just don't quite belong in the Church at all.* This sentiment is shared by so many alternative, smart sounding, stylish and new Church movements today. These movements often identify themselves as those who are not really being part of the mainstream Church. What does that really mean? This awkward unsustainable sentiment is the lostness of orphanhood where adoption into the family is never quite complete because the Father's love is never fully received. So even though many Christians love Jesus they still view themselves as second class citizens in the kingdom and are unable to find a comfortable integration with any of the rest of Church—the people of God.

It is not enough to find our identity in what we are not, believers, it is time to find our identity in who we really are.

This is a symptom of orphanism that we should help one another learn to discern well so we can bring the love of the Father into full view. If one symptom of the orphan's struggle with identity is found in self-diminishment, then another is strongly related: it is the inability to receive honor for a job well done.

Our Father God loves us so much that he is always looking for ways to celebrate us. Just like an earthly parent our God is looking for ways to bake us a cake, throw us a party, or take pictures of us in that special moment when we have achieved. Though an orphan may stand on the winners platform and receive the award there may remain in them an uncomfortable inner voice that says, "I don't really deserve this."

Remember, if an orphan is never sure of his place in the heart of the Father, then standing in a place of honor can feel fraudulent rather than glorious. Sons can stand and receive, but orphans will have trouble. When accolades and honor come the lost-orphan's way—though these honors are coveted—the feelings of being undeserving can be crushing. This inability to be praised or honored stems from constant feelings of unworthiness. Honor will always feel like an undeserved favor to the heart of the orphan who doesn't really believe they are worthy of the great favor of God. Being a son, however, is the greatest favor in God's eyes we could ever achieve. It is the ultimate place on the winner's podium. The Father's pride explodes all over us as sons. If we are confident in his love for us then we can stand and receive it, but if we doubt—even a little—receiving his loving gestures may be very awkward. It may find us pushing our way to the corner of the room so as not to be noticed. The orphan spirit says, "Someone else must deserve this more than me."

Again, the orphan struggles to be confident and relaxed in their true identity as sons. As leaders we have to commit to speaking into the hearts of those we love and reminding them of who they really are. This can be as simple as being very direct when we compliment others because we are aware that some will struggle. Instead of saying simply, *Thanks, that was a great job!* which sounds awesome in and of itself, but with wisdom we go the extra mile and we say, "You know I appreciate you for more than what you do, but I have to say, 'Thanks' because you did a great job. I am not worried about your pride swelling up, or about how you might think you could have done it better. I think you are perfect. Thanks for being my friend." Don't think that was laying it on too heavy. If we don't learn how to defeat the lies of the enemy by laying the truth down deep into the hearts of those we love we will just have to try and help them heal more later. This is the encouraging work of preventive ministry that seeks to strategically draw up and recognize sonship in everyone.

CHRISTIAN ORPHANS WANDER

Wandering is pretty easy to identify. It is the evidence that a person is looking for a *place* to find fulfillment because they don't know they have a permanent place in the heart of the Father. This orphan spirit needs to know that Jesus has prepared a place for them, but in the meantime they wander.

Have you met the person in their twenties who has attended three colleges, has two degrees, changes jobs every twelve months, changes pursuits every eighteen months, and who is always talking about what they are going to do next? This may be a sign of youthful experimentation, but it may also be the wandering orphan spirit at work. Can you tell the difference?

I have a friend of over twenty-five years who has had a life long struggle with looking for a place. He could never feel satisfied in his work or in his relationships. He confessed to me, that he has felt like a wanderer his whole life. He was born into a Baptist minister's family, did every Christian thing that could be done, and played in a Christian rock band when he was in college. When God started walking Scott into his sonship he felt the need to travel to Europe and reconnect with his estranged father who had a disastrous affair with the church secretary and left his ministry career over twenty years ago. Obviously, that left my friend struggling with his own place in the world and with his natural father. During this visit his dad pulled out some old VHS movies they made when Scott was a kid. He saw a video of his father holding him on his lap and kissing him and cooing over him with love when he was just a little boy. He recounted to me on the phone that he had never, not once, remembered his father touching him and loving him like that. Because of that trip and the images on that video he had a breakthrough with his natural dad which gave way to a breakthrough with his spiritual Dad. Now he is beginning to mature as a son. For the first time in 20 years Scott is beginning to lead his conversations and thoughts not with striving and looking for a place, but in learning to enjoy the place he occupies in the Father's heart. What a major life shift. If this is the impact of reconciling with our natural fathers just imagine the impact of reconciling with our heavenly Father!

Another symptom that reveals the wandering-orphan is the inability to receive the love of *the fathers*. At the very opening of the book we noted that the question, "Who is your spiritual father?" could be taken cosmically toward our belief in God, but it could also be applied to our acceptance of spiritual parents in this life. We should not find the idea of spiritual fathers awkward at all. Paul was clear with the Church in Corinth that "Even though you have ten thousand guardians in Christ, you do not have many fathers" (1 Corinthian 4:15). Paul recognized in this entire group a willingness to receive managers, to receive counselors, to receive overseers of every kind—but they could not receive the fathers. This was a problem for orphan Christians then, and it is a problem now.

The orphan spirit has great difficulty receiving the love of a spiritual father because it is so foreign, and so seemingly unbelievable. In the natural this love might even be seen as a manipulation or a control method. After all, an orphan coming out of an orphanage might have learned that all the methods the overseers used were the manipulative, temporary controls that were necessary to bring order to chaos, but they were all short lived and never coming from a parental commitment. In other words, there was no lasting family love. Because of this hurt many well-intentioned spiritual parents' actions have been mistaken for manipulation as they gently place their hands on the shoulder of a believer only to see this person recoil in horror assuming the very worst of intentions. Why the flashback? Because the hurt memories from manipulative managers are real.

If we know that Christian orphans are lost and wandering, and we realize that they may fear the tools of management, then we have to be wise and awake when we move forward to love them. We must be committed to helping them, however, and not choose to be passive just to avoid any tensions. Leaders, we must grow more aware that our best intentions for nurturing others cannot be received if the hurts and judgements of the orphan heart still filters their vision at every turn. We must coach forgiveness toward the managers who undeservedly assumed the place of father before us. We must make long term commitments to those we love and prove over time that we are not temporary, and our love is not a trick to garner service from others. If we are going to be excellent at pastoring, then we must help the wandering-orphan receive the Father's love and come home to the family.

CHRISTIAN ORPHANS NEED A HOME

The orphan spirit is naturally attracted to organizations with great style and vision. The organizations with the best projects, the most benevolent works, and the best opportunities for securing a place of honor will hold the most attraction for the orphan mindset. These are modern institutions of clear shape and size like the hip local church, the passionate missions or prayer organization, or the notable university.

I stood in front of a wonderful group of young people a little while back who were part of a missions and prayer organization. Now the mission of the organization was brilliant and the leaders and people were all beautiful, but I could tell something was out of order. The orphan spirit pervaded the atmosphere as young people were looking for places, and leaders were struggling for the right management style, and their was a lot of uncertainty about who was leading *what* to *where*. At a large gathering I asked the question, "For how many of you is this organization the second or even third missions organization you have been a part of in the last two years?"

The answer came when over half of the room of around 100 people raised their hands.

I said in affect, "People, I love you, but it is time to come into your sonship and quit wandering the earth in search of the perfect orphanage in which you will finally feel purposeful and valuable."

The ministry time of repentance and prayer was absolutely astounding. At present, this organization is on a massive internal reformation as it returns to its original family identity—instead of becoming another missionary ideal looking for members.

Many other orphans looking for orphanages find the university a favorite place to remain, and many remain life-long. The reason for this life long appeal is that the university is a place of infinite opportunities for recognition and awards, places and promotions. Grades are handed out regularly, favorite professors can be claimed, and favorite spots on the totem pole can be secured. Furthermore, in academia we are free to talk about intimacy and pontificate about family without ever being scrutinized for our lack of participation in either.

Please, please pause and make this note: I am not saying, nor have I meant to imply, that everyone who goes back to college, or attends a local fellowship, or joins a mission organization is an orphan. That is nuts. I need to directly confront those thoughts and remind you that this book is not a handbook for the spiritually thoughtless. You must discern these things yourself. I simply can't divide you and every single person in your life down to one unrealistically confining category. Remember, we are talking about the influences of wrong beliefs in people's lives, not the need to harshly categorize beautifully complicated human beings into a single psychoanalytical box.

The truth remains: the orphanage is a place of shelter for the orphan heart, and until they discover a place in the family of God which is relational, loving, and true then there will be little alternative than to build and belong to the best orphanages man can construct. Can you discern the difference between enjoying the practical helps of an organization, and trusting in it as an orphanage for the heart?

CHRISTIAN ORPHANS STRIVE

What we mean by *strive* is that the Christian orphan in some way believes that anything he has is the result of his effort and not really the gift of God. Therefore, the Christian orphan will constantly struggle with fear of financial loss and ruin and will find himself grasping for resources whenever he can. Seriously, how could any believer walk in confidence concerning their provision (regardless of how often they listen to financial coaches on the radio) if they do not know that God's Fathering heart is to provide for them as his sons no matter what? The great warfare of generous giving must be waged against the lies of the devil to overcome this false belief and false habit of thinking. I will explain.

To help us all avoid thinking that the orphan spirit is synonymous with a Christian loser or a "backslider" (for the southern protestant) let me tell you about one of my spiritual sons. He is a man of great insight as a teacher, a confident husband and father, an accomplished musician, and has a heart for the kingdom of God. Yet, at times, this friend struggled to the point of despair over one issue—the issue of finances. It was easy to tell what day of the week he had worked to balance his bank books because of his diminished heart and depressed countenance. In a meeting on the porch, under the aspen trees, he confessed, "Ben, I feel like every time the question of financial lack comes up that I fall into a hole."

I responded in the only way I knew how that would offer some help. I said, "Until you prove to yourself that God loves you enough to take care of you, and that you deserve to be taken care of because you are a son, then there will be nothing else I can really say or do to help you."

That sponsored a new conversation about who God really was to him when it came down to provision, and some new insights were gained in that moment.

I said to him and his wife, "You guys need to pull $500 bucks out of your bank right now (this was, by the way, the figure that they needed for some other bill that had been killing their sense of having *enough*), divide it up, and bless five people regardless of whether they needed it or not. This, dear reader, is called *putting it in the devil's face*. This is spiritual warfare. We can defeat the lies of the enemy by rolling over on top of them with the truth. This couple waged that war of generosity, and they broke free of the chains of doubt and depression related to finances to this day. Can you discern when your friends are struggling against the internal voices of orphanhood?

Leaders, if we are to help those struggling with the orphan spirit we have to become great at sensing the grasping for resources, and we have to learn that defensiveness and positional obsessions are sure to come. Another symptom of the striving heart is defensiveness. The defensive-orphan heart is in the life of the zealous leader who ascends the food chain of leadership through seminary, associate pastoral positions, and then finally the senior pastorate only to live there as a high control obsessive who is constantly on the lookout for threats to his position. I have seen this in fellowship leaders both young and old. The fear comes from the internal belief that his role is the result of hard work and gifting and is not intrinsically his because God has loved him and created him for the work of the ministry. Whole systems of voting for "pastors" and firing fellowship leaders have grown up around this false belief system to influence the leadership pathologies of entire denominations. These leaders will have complex methods of defending their position and their authority. We must look for it in ourselves, and help others see it as well.

This kind of orphan-leader will always view the people in his care as those to be managed and directed, impressed and soothed. This is in no way connected to the heart of the fathers. Many seminaries, I have heard, even teach young pastors to avoid intimacy with their congregations in order to avoid unnecessary conflict or expectations. I have heard that sad news more than once. This, of course, is nothing more than professional orphans training bright, young impressionable orphans how to survive as new leaders of the spiritual orphanage. This is also a crime against the family of God.

This idea of securing a position using personal effort and skill leads the orphan-leader to engage in all kinds of political dramas and will lead him to view his work in a fellowship through that lens. Not too long ago I watched a young leader rise to his "senior pastor" position by organizing a revolt with the fellowship's board to throw out the previous senior pastor of seven years with little warning, no discussion, and a couple weeks severance pay. After that "justified reorganization" he was asked by a friend what he thought ministry really was. His answer was telling. He said he saw the church as a chess game and all the people were the chess pieces. His role as the pastor, according to his orphan-insight, was to move the people-pieces into the places he needed them to be, to keep order for their benefit, and help them accomplish things for God. Apparently, for him, sacrificing a less than desirable chess piece was justified by his views of how the game-board should look to him. Now tell me, how would you like to be a chess piece, I mean, member of his congregation?

Leaders, we must repent from the orphanage models we have supported or been a part of, and choose to receive the love of the Father and his call to become family leaders! We were meant to be lovers of a family, not managers of institutions. We are going to have to announce that to our people.

Men, we are called to father.

Women, we are called to mother.

As leaders we will do whatever that means and whatever that takes—because it is our true nature. I do not set people in places of authority when I can discern they are filled with striving and defensiveness. It will not be good for them or for those they are trying to serve. This might seem a little harsh at first glance, but I believe in this particular manifestation of the immature heart it is prudent that leaders with a heart for the family protect themselves and their watchcare by carefully, and lovingly, restricting the authority of those who are really having trouble with this striving orphan spirit.

CHRISTIAN ORPHANAGES

There is no greater crime among leadership than to prop up the orphan spirit—yet we continue to find ways to do it. Mostly, I believe we do it because we don't know any better. It seems as though we have been trying to weave our lives and instincts as orphans into our new lives as sons with no decided effort to root it out. It is not working. It is oil and water. I will include myself right in the middle of this challenge as I have been painfully guilty of the following three crimes against believers that we must all now put to an end. This section is specifically designed to give you, the leader, some practical challenges to break out of old orphan-leadership modes.

Just like the crimes that sometimes pervade a culture until there is a great public outcry these three crimes have begun to make the evening news in Christian's lives everywhere. We can either be caught on grainy video tape as conspirators in the ongoing tragedy ... or we can lead in the march to change the system.

IS THE ORPHANAGE OUR GOOD NEWS?

If the work of Christ in its entirety is to adopt us into a real spiritual family, why then would we ever choose to build and live in orphanages?

It seems that Christians everywhere believe in the Gospel of the Orphanage. We have been inviting others to come and join, come and sit, come and agree, come and be a member of this thing or that thing for centuries. This kind of Church meeting is a place where we get together and hear messages of hope, and teachings of Godly order. In our Church meetings we offer a temporary relief from the chaos of this orphan-filled world. This is not the gospel of adoption to sonship, this is the gospel of temporary shelter, some spiritual food, and some spiritual clothing. For some this seems to be enough. I wonder why?

I think it goes something like this: When we receive the love of Christ we are adopted in the family of God and we become related to other family members as brothers, sisters, mothers, fathers, uncles, etc. However, and unfortunately, most of us enter a form of religion where we gather together in buildings and organizations that we mistakenly, and unfortunately call Church. We do this, by the way, even though Jesus never called a building or an organization the Church, and neither did any of the apostles and prophets.

The tradition of going to a meeting of people and calling it *Church* teaches us to get accustomed to the orphanage life and we learn to call it and the people that meet there: *family*. Though our hearts are crying out for true family where we know God as Father and one another as sister, uncle, father, son, etc., many of us find our relational surroundings to be filled with teachers, fellow journeymen, meetings, servants, partners, projects, managers, directors, volunteers and employees ... all of which build in us a tragic way of viewing this institutionalized world of management and crowd control as our Christian family. Isn't it a tragic idea to think of those who actually have a real spiritual family still choosing to live in an orphanage and call it family? Yet, we see it all the time, and many of us are living it right now. Paul echoed this tragedy when he said to the Corinthian believers in 1 Corinthians 4:15, "Even though you have ten thousand guardians in Christ, you do not have many fathers."

Do you feel this way about your journey with God now? If so, let me encourage you directly: you can be free from this impersonal touch, this institutional life, and you can come into a full realization of the joy of family! We can be Family in God and with one another, and I will share with you some practical ways to begin.

First, leaders, it is time to repent for building orphanages. It is time to build up believers into the family where they belong. We must repent from trying to build the forms and programs that look good so that people will come to them, and we must start building up believers into the sons that God has called them to be according to Ephesians 4:12 where it says concerning the purpose of leadership that we are, "to prepare God's people for works of service, so that the body of Christ may be built up." It does not say we are to build the Church, promote the Church, or preach the Church. It says we are to equip and train believers, the saints, to take up their own responsibilities in the family of God. When believers become mature in Christ then the Church which is a family of relationships simply grows as a by-product. The kingdom family is proclaimed first, then the Church is growing effortlessly in its wake. We will speak more on this later, but for now a good start is to write out the names of a few people you actually pastor (and not just address during a weekly meeting) and start calling them the Church instead of the building you meet in, and then decide that helping them mature in Christ is the dead-center of your work.

Secondly, leaders, it is time to repent for being managers instead of fathers. Remember, an orphanage is a place where children can be brought off the street to live together and be nurtured by a team of people who are functioning in some way as surrogate parents—but mostly as managers of a crowd. Now in an orphanage we normally find people who don't know who their parents are and so they must live this way in order to find some nurture and some care. We can see that the world is full of institutions, social forms and fraternities, religious systems, and political identities that serve as orphanages. These orphanages are places where the fatherless can find some sense of belonging. This is, tragically, where many of us as Church leaders have become trapped as we agreed to bring our old orphan ways into the new ways of kingdom family.

A voice came to us and said, "Yes, God has adopted you just as the Holy Spirit is convincing you, but your only hope for family is really to just live and learn inside of this institution ... this is the orphanage where you must grow, find, and make your own family ... there is nothing more." And this is where we have chosen to stay. We have been here so long that we now call organizations and gatherings *Churches* because it is all we have known. We have lost sight, and lost heart for anything more. A great way to regain our perspective and to begin restoring family to our work is to take that same list of people you already put together and go to them individually with this heart and these words, "I love you like a son, and I want to be a better spiritual father to you." You might think using the word *father* here is frightening or over-reaching. I don't. I think it establishes the willingness to love and treat someone with deep, personal respect. I think the word is full of long-term, family commitment. I think we have been trained to avoid this kind of personal commitment in our institutions, and therefore we have to take great risks and add some drama to our language in order to help us overcome! Rather than settle for cold, managing language which trains us to never take any personal risk, why not try and use some family language and see what happens. I am not, to be very clear, asking those of you with manager's hearts to start using family language. This is tragic and criminal. I am releasing those of you who have kingdom hearts for the people of God to no longer fear your familial identity.

Leaders it is time to father our people into their destiny as sons, instead of just managing them out of their present chaos. This is old, institutional style leadership at its best: calm the waves, don't rock the boat, downplay the storm—it, too, shall pass. Time doesn't heal, but a fathering love can.

When we say we are called to father, we are not saying that we are taking the fathering role of God away from him or that we are assuming a new position of cultic power. No. What we are saying is that there is a profound difference in the heart and tools of a father as compared to the heart and tools of the manager and it is time to act in a way in keeping with family instead of the low risk modes of running a business. Fathers risk their lives and their reputations on the children they love and they are never willing to negotiate a present, contrived peace in exchange for long term pain and failure in the lives of their sons.

THE FAILURE TO THRIVE SYNDROME

After we repent from our work of building orphanages it is time to repent for the second crime we have committed against the people of God: the failure to touch them.

Our new kingdom DNA needs family in order to come to life. I said new kingdom DNA, because "if anyone is in Christ, he is a new creation; the old has gone, the new has come!" (2 Corinthians 5:17). You see, when we receive Christ he brings us the life of God and transforms us from the inside out. Now, we simply need to be in the right environment to grow. We will mature and grow best inside of a loving family. Real families touch and care for one another.

A Harvard Medical study was performed on babies in an overcrowded Romanian orphanage. Researchers found that babies who went hours without touch had high levels of cortisol (a hormone activated by high stress levels), lower immune systems and an overall decline in their health. In other words, babies who were not personally touched and cared for were failing to thrive. Every baby is meant to be loved, touched and cared for by a caring parent. When babies fail to receive this kind of touch they suffered from what the researchers came to term the *Failure To Thrive Syndrome*.

These untouched babies could survive, but they would not thrive.

What is true in the natural is true in the spiritual. If we go on believing that the institution of meetings is all there is, then we will go on learning to survive, but we will not thrive as kingdom sons.

Every believer who comes to God as a *new creation* deserves the loving touch of other believers and those who would love them as spiritual parents. Without this kind of nurturing, personal love these believers will fail. I say *fail* not because I am trying to predict their destruction, but because I am trying to confront a reality we already see as an epidemic in our fellowships around the world: people come to Christ, make a public profession of their trust in him, and then in great numbers slowly fade away from ever being seen again. A great number of local fellowships seem to cycle through predictable modulations of growth, success, difficulty, demise, and dormancy with great predictability. There is no reason to blame the evil culture around us for this continuing problem when it is mostly the result, I believe, of the *Failure To Thrive Syndrome* at work. We have failed as leaders in our commitment to touch those we care for. Many of us don't have a clue of even how to go about it.

How can we continue to focus on preaching the Good News of the Orphanage and expect new believers to thrive in it? Why do we continue to ask people to attend meetings, join our churches, and assimilate into our organizations without any higher expectation than their basic survival? Don't we know that everyone deserves personal touch and personal care?

Maybe this has been the only kind of Church ministry we have ever known and so it is the only kind we are able to share. Maybe if we have been raised in an orphanage ourselves then this is just the best that we could do. We can begin to break out! One way to begin to break out of this cycle is to call someone on your list of spiritual family connections and say, "Can we go hiking this afternoon for an hour or so? I would like to spend time just listening to what is on your heart."

Don't be mistaken, I am not singing the "small Church is the only good Church" song. That is not true. It is not any less logical than believing that a small orphanage is going to produce sonship any better than a large one. The deciding factor in the quality of our lives is always relational, it is never material or structural. You see, size and system has nothing to do with the real need of our hearts. What we need is not a better system, what we need is the spirit of the family of God coming alive in personal touch and personal commitment to one another along family lines.

Dear ones, there is no judgement coming from my heart towards anyone who has suffered under this orphanage culture. I have learned this hard lesson personally over many years of suffering. I have had to walk through the fires of the harsh shock of these two cultures, family kingdom and orphanage, colliding in real time. We are all in this together. We must all repent from the fear of risking intimacy, and decide to come out of the impersonal madness of the Gospel of the Orphanage and decide to live into something totally different—totally family.

COMMUNITY IS A POOR REPLACEMENT

If the second crime against the Church has been living in isolation from one another, then the third crime against the Church that we must repent of is the crime of preaching the Gospel of Community.

Now, I would like to take this moment to delineate between the Gospel of the kingdom and the Gospel of Community. The latter seems to be the hottest buzzword in Christianity today. It is used in a wholly good-hearted way to try and bring people together. However, it is, as many orphans have learned, only a partial answer.

The word *community* is found in the Bible but only in scripture referring to Israel. There are two Hebrew words. Both words share the meaning of *assembly* or *community*, with the distinction that one is used when referring to Israel assembled for religious ceremony, and the second is used usually in denoting a unique collection of people in a place like in Gen. 28:3, "May God Almighty bless you and make you fruitful and increase your numbers until you become a community of peoples." It is used one time in the New Testament, but only in reference to the Jews as a unique people group living in a particular place. That is to say when a bunch of Jewish families lived together in a single place their collection was called a community. This word *community*, both in Biblical language and in modern usage, is just a common, generic word that identifies a collection of peoples in the same place. This is important to note because in Scripture Abraham's family, is never promoted, first, as a community. The people of God are always seen, first, as a *family*.

As the people of God today, we are to be seen as a family first, and then when we gather together in a place we can be called a community. The problem with the modern *community* buzz-hype is that community is proclaimed first and we are developing a backwards hope that family will pop out of it. It does not happen this way, it never has happened that way, and it never will happen that way.

If we are driving in our car and through our front windshield we are driving toward a land called *Family*, then we can look in our rearview mirror and see community developing naturally behind us. But if we drive that same car of purpose and fill our forward vision with a land called *Community* we will become disappointed and frustrated because we will not see Family developing as a natural by-product. We will, unfortunately, in the latter situation where we are driving toward community, see division, burn-out, and egos running wild.

We all know that this is really what community is: families and peoples gathered into a place who learn to work and live together. This is a common thing, a basic thing. Did you notice where the word *family* was in that simple definition? It was right up at the front. Family always comes first. We used to think that all of those "begat" Scriptures were a waste of good Bible paper until we realized that the Father is all about family! These genealogies, and family connections, and these father and son narratives make up the backbone of his plan.

Lineages are never footnotes or fillers in a Father's heart.

He does not try to get us all to live together, or to agree on everything, or to assign us to the same public work project. He simply adopts us and then, well, we are his family. We have one Father. We all become related together in an instant. When we pursue this family life, then community will grow as a beautiful and natural by-product just like healthy families can make great neighborhoods.

Readers, listen carefully. When believers who grow up in a spiritual orphanage hear someone preaching the Gospel of Community they will have a great natural attraction to it. It sounds like a wonderful upgrade to orphanage life. Orphans will join community faster than any other new form of organization, but it will become nothing more than an upgraded orphanage if they learn nothing more of family intimacy. Yes, it is a difficult emotional transition for those whose entire Christian walk has been lived in impersonal institutional settings, and being asked to connect to others in personal and intimate family ways is going to be hard. Maybe someone could win the argument that the Gospel of Community is at least a kind of half-way house. I understand. I don't have condemnation for anyone who would make that point. I just do not want anyone to trade in *excellent* for *good* as an eternal substitute.

Friends don't let friends drive drunk, and family members don't let other family members stay in orphanages. We must claim one another personally! This doesn't require abandoning buildings, or dumping traditions, as some have been quick to proclaim. I think this is missing the point. What the kingdom requires of us is something a hundred times more courageous, and a thousand times more noble. It will require that we receive the Father's love, walk in our sonship, and claim our spiritual family ... one by one, and without regard to where they meet, what they do, or where they live. Changing structure may not be important. Changing how we related to those within the structure is of supreme importance.

Leaders, it is time to learn how to claim personal relationships and call them family connections. We must learn how to respect and honor one another, love and help one another, and relate together in a way that reflects our family DNA. We must fight for family, and allow the beauty of community to grow as a byproduct. It is time to begin to claim our spiritual family as part of our inheritance. We must begin to name aloud our fathers, and sisters, and daughters in our spiritual family. That's right, a very practical way to begin to build family is to simply look at that list of names you have already written and say aloud, "These are members of my spiritual family. I claim them as my own." This kind of claiming is a far cry from believing that everyone who sits down in your Bible study class with you for an hour on Sunday mornings are necessarily close spiritual family connections for you. This kind of claiming will be the beginning of our journey as leaders of family first, and the transformation of our Church culture from orphanage to family home!

SLAVE

WHO IS A SLAVE?

There are many kinds of slaves both in the natural and in the spiritual. There are freed slaves who walk the street, and there are captive slaves who belong to a single master. Some slaves have benevolent, good hearted masters, and some have hateful, exploitative masters. Some are born into slavery, some are sold in, and others actually opt-in in order to avoid a life with no provision at all. Some slaves find their enslavement to be an unbearable oppression while some find it an unavoidable condition.

Though slavery is now recognized as a global human rights issue as noted in Article 4 of the Universal Declaration of Human Rights: "No one shall be held in slavery or servitude; slavery and the slave trade shall be prohibited in all their forms," slavery, nonetheless, is still a global issue. No matter what research is referenced those in slavery around the globe reach into the millions.

Some slaves live under the forced labor called peonage or debt bondage, some slaves are under contract as indentured servants, others are considered chattel slaves where they are nothing more than the property of their masters. In recent years, and it should not go unsaid, the numbers of people especially women and children who are sold into sex slavery has become increasingly epidemic. The modern slave trade is called human trafficking, or in this instance sex trafficking, and it may be the most inhumane, repulsive kind of slavery ever committed by the human race. Whatever the case, slaves all share a basic definition: Slaves are owned and directed by someone else, and they work in order to be valuable.

Just as we noted in the first section of this book on orphanhood, we will be speaking in general terms. I am not an expert on slavery, nor can I speak authoritatively about every detail of enslavement historically or for the present. We will give ourselves permission to speak inside of the broadest generalizations, and simplest facts related to the common state of slavery. We do so in part because we are all human beings and as such we can use our common human imagination to understand others at the same time we are discovering our own hearts. By doing this we will be able to wrap our minds around the basics of slavery in the natural, and this will help us accomplish our goals in understanding slavery in the spiritual. In this section of the book our ultimate goal is to define spiritual slavery so we can identify it in ourselves and in the lives of those we love. We see it as a tragic brokenness when believers still think and act live slaves even though they have no reason to remain that way. It needs to be repaired.

I recently saw a film about the famous British parlamentarian, William Wilburforce. It is a gripping real life drama about a man who lived in a time when slavery was an acceptable part of commerce. It was just business in the eyes of mainstream culture. But in the middle of this cultural acceptance Wilburforce got a glimpse of the slave as a person and in an instant could no longer be anything other than a champion for the freedom of all slaves. For him the situation became personal. For him the condition became criminal. He is now known as one of the greatest *abolitionists* because of his work to abolish slavery in his time.

There is a call in this book for each of us take up a similar call and to become abolitionists of spiritual slavery.

THE SLAVE'S WORLD VIEW

The following things are generally true about the mindset of slaves.

SLAVES WORK FOR A PLACE

The only position that a slave can hold is the place his master assigns to him.

Slavery is often the desperate solution for a people who see no other way to survive. We find this to be the case among the Hebrew people under the government of the Egyptian Pharaohs of the Old Testament. After years of famine in their own land the people had traded their money, their livestock and all they had in order to buy food and survive. Finally, they came and said, "There is nothing left for our lord except our bodies and our land. Why should we perish before your eyes—we and our land as well? Buy us and our land in exchange for food, and we with our land will be in bondage to Pharaoh" (from Genesis 47:18-19).

After that kind of contract is made then all rights have been given over to the one who will extract payment from the slave personally using any provisions or helps the slave might render. Every part of the slave's life, then, is dependent on the will of his owner and the work he requires. The only place the slave has, in others words, is whatever place he occupies in the mind of the owner.

And how does a slave earn a place?

A slave earns a place through hard work and noteworthy usefulness. For young capable slaves this proposition may seem advantageous in some ways, but the harsh reality in this equation is, of course, that when a slave is no longer useful, then that slave no longer has a place in the mind of the master and no longer has a source of provision. A slave's place can be lost and therefore he must always work to gain it and keep it. For the slave it is simple: work and you will receive food and provision as a reward, don't work and you will receive nothing.

We can easily see this process in the life of the chattel slave who was bought and owned in order to labor in the mines, the fields, and the homes of slave owners. This slave's whole life and sense of personal value was charted out on a scale of usefulness. In broader, but in more subtle terms, we can also see this mindset develop in a people whose government sees its citizenry under the obligation to pay taxes because their work is a duty to the state so that the state might spend it on whom they wish, but especially to take care of the unproductive. The most useful workers in this society will be rewarded and given benefits during the useful years of their lives, while the older and infantile members of society will be seen as less valuable because they are less productive and therefore become a drain on the system. The trouble has been that the balance of producers versus takers always shifts toward the takers over time. This is not a book on economics, but it might be one on the economics of the human experience, and so it is worth pointing out that this is how the initial benevolent tones of socialism evolve quietly into the soul-killing enslavement of whole nations of people under the direction of a few. Indeed, there are educated countries today where, in the people's mindset, the tax burdens have reached just such a burdensome level, but their dependence on the government is still unquenchable so they say, just as the Hebrews said, "There is nothing left for our lord except our bodies and our land."

SLAVES COMPETE

Every slave is in fierce competition with other slaves to achieve a place in this world.

Remember, the place we refer to is a place in the mind of the slave's owner, but this sense of place is transferred to the slaves in their view of one another. Slave owners must look over their stock of workers and assess who has capacity to accomplish what kind of work and give rewards and punishments accordingly. Each slave will learn to quickly self-assess his place on the scale of usefulness as he judges himself and others in light of his master's own system of judgement. Jesus warns us in Luke 6 that judgement always leads to more judgement. It is a kind of yeast in the bread of slave culture: comparison, judgement, and competition.

Now the slave's ability to self-judge becomes essential because it helps him measure his own place of usefulness and it provides him an assurance for his provision and favor. A slave must know his place on the ladder. It builds a system of expectation in his life. If he excels in his competition then he will be rewarded. If he fails in his competitions then he can predict the removal of provision and favor. This leads to two intertwined but conflicting instincts in slave culture: one is passive and one is aggressive. One is to create social justice or equilibrium, and the other is to over-achieve and find reward. These two instincts are, just as they seem, in opposition. This is one reason the slave's world is so full of tension and frustrations. The desire to seek both equilibrium and notoriety, simultaneously, is a careful science in the land of slavery based solely on *who is looking*.

The first instinct in slave culture is to equalize the playing field among the slaves so that punishment can be avoided. This is a passive response to the fear of punishment. This is exactly why in a slave culture the overachievers will not be rewarded among the slaves themselves. Have you ever wondered why, in school, it is so natural among the students to mock and tease the overachievers in the classroom? Why is anti-achievement a universal instinct in grade school? Why don't they all give praise as a community for those among them who excel and do well? Simple. The overachievers threaten everyone's place of acceptance and favor on the scale of approval. These overachievers "blow the curve" on this scale for the rest of the class. They extend the scale of self-judgement and make it more difficult to earn a place not only on report cards, but in the heart of the teacher and anyone who examines the scale of achievement. This is why in slave culture the status quo is the place to be if you are a slave, and social pressures will be applied to pull down the overachievers so that there is a bigger portion of "average" performance. The underachievers, on the other hand, will always be allowed to remain because they are the very reason the average can be rewarded with favor and honor because, "At least we are better than those guys" which provides safety in the slave-society. Slaves seek equilibrium when they are surrounded by the eyes and attention of other slaves.

Secondly, slave culture is filled with aggressive competition. We must remember that there is only so much room in any one place. With limited room and more slaves than room there is going to be some heated competition. There are many kinds of places that slaves compete for. A place might be the recognition as being the most faithful at a job. The place might be wearing the medal for the best performance in a particular work. It might be the reputation as the fiercest defender of the owner's honor, or the arbiter of order in a given situation. That's right, slaves can even earn a special place in the mind of the master by taking on the role and heart of the master and acting as an arm of enforcement. This is a very special place. This is the classic boss-and-henchman scenario that we see played out in endless versions of movie scripts, and it is the real life scenario of slaves.

What it all forms into is the culture of slavery, and the culture of slavery is defined by the word *competition,* but this competition takes place when the slave perceives the eye of the master is measuring him. The heart of a slave says to itself, "I will do anything to advance so that I can secure myself a place in the heart of my master and, therefore, secure my place of provision."

If this places the slave in direct competition with friend or family, then it becomes the law of the animal kingdom at that point and only the strong will survive. We begin, then, with Darwin's natural selection being played out in the culture of slavery as the best workers and competitors are singled out for reward, but over time we end with Spencer's theory of the *survival of the fittest* as those who continually fail are eventually done away with.

It might be easy to make generalizations about the co-laboring philosophies of socialism and capitalism again in relationship to the passive and aggressive ways that slaves seek to provide for themselves, but again, this is not a book that could handle that. Let's just say, in light of the obvious here, that the heart of slaves will struggle to live in health, joy, and contentment regardless of what socio-economic system they toil under.

SLAVES FEAR PUNISHMENT

Slaves have no permanent place in the heart of their master so they live in constant fear of failure and punishment.

Punishment contains with in it a necessary amount of pain. No one looks forward to pain, and so the fear of punishment itself has a tremendous power to control someone. A slave owner uses punishment—and the fear of punishment—as his primary tool to deter his slaves from undesirable action. This pain inflicted from a master to a slave is designed to prevent the recurrence of an undesirable action. Punishment, or discipline in this sense, is not like revenge or retribution because it has a component that involves changing a person's future direction. It is not just retribution.

Now here is the challenge to consider. People in every nation and culture use punishment as a parenting tool. Punishment is, for all practical purposes, a routine way of guiding children to not repeat an undesirable action. Obviously some punishments are considered abusive as they are totally out of the bounds of decency and civility towards children. What those boundaries are, in exact terms, are not the subject of this book, but we could propose that punishment ranging from the removal or playground privileges to a painful swat to the bottom-side of an uncooperative child are going to be in general operation all over the world as acceptable punishments to train children to obey the rules of acceptable behavior.

It is a Proverb often quoted from the Old Testament that says, "Do not withhold discipline [punishment with the future in mind] from a child; if you punish him with the rod [spanking], he will not die. Punish him with the rod and save his soul from death" (Proverbs 23:13-14). This is the basis for understanding a useful version of what we call corporal punishment. Though spanking children has fallen out of favor in popular culture especially when administered by a non-parent, the notion that children don't need to be punished for bad behavior is a myth of epic proportions and proofs. A child who lives with no painful consequences for bad behavior is usually not a child that anyone wants to live near when he becomes an adult. Even in the New Testament the writer of Hebrews says that God punishes his own sons, "because the Lord disciplines those he loves, and he punishes everyone he accepts as a son" (Hebrews 12:6).

The challenge is this: what is the difference between being punished as a slave, and being punished as a child?

The answer is *family love.*

This is the reason I can say that non-familial, unloving spanking may be no good for any man, but familial, loving spanking may be for the good of all mankind.

Where there is no love *punishment* is a diminishing, dehumanizing act. It is calculated revenge and legal retribution.

Punishment with the absence of family love should be feared and it should be seen as repulsive. Even the punishment of criminals by imprisonment is known to be, on its own, nothing more than the temporary isolation of a broken person away from society where he proved he could not function. The society he joins in prison will probably not rehabilitate him and so the managers of society hope that base fear of the punishment will be a working deterrent. The use of pain will have no boundaries when administered without love. But where there is love and a deep heart connection with a person's future—when there is a deep commitment to the development of a person's character with the most loving and caring of motives—then focused punishment becomes a welcome tool for both the father and the son. Love limits the pain, and focuses the act of discipline toward the child's healthy future. In the heart of a son who knows his father loves him the consequences of punishment are actually a welcome expression of his father's desire to build in him strength and maturity. It is a sincere expression that the father is, indeed, paying attention and is committed even through calculated, appropriate punishment to stay involved with his son. 1 John 4:18 puts it perfectly, "There is no fear in love. But perfect love drives out fear, because fear has to do with punishment. The one who fears is not made perfect in love."

However, it remains that for the slave punishment is only fueled by fear because there is no such family love. There is no lifelong commitment to the slave's well being and to his future; there is only the selfish, self serving desire of the master to get the work he wants completed.

SLAVES NEED DIRECTION

A slave has no compass that points to his intrinsic, eternal value. This value-compass for the slave is an external one that measures him according to how he is valued by others.

In the view of the ownership-master class this is a self-perpetuating system of judgement where they say, "You are no one unless I tell you you are someone," and "If I didn't tell you, then you wouldn't even know who you are." The master can develop a sense of benevolence in this judgement system because he actually rescues his slaves from lostness by telling them who they are and what they are worth. Then the master can confidently say, "I have you, slave, and I know that you are unable to actually live a life in freedom without further direction and training. I will show my good heart and now give you the training you need to survive." This is a true statement in the system of slaves. This division of the world into *those who need to direct*, and *those who need to be directed* is the root of much prejudice in many nations around the world where whole races of peoples are now viewed as a subclass of human beings, and in some countries whole electorates are viewed as sheep in need of a governmental shepherd.

Master classes have assessed others to be inferior and in need of direction, and slave classes have agreed to the assessment. That's right: this point of view is not exclusive to the ownership-master class. Slaves, themselves, learn to see themselves and their personal value only in terms related to their need to be directed. Given, this can be a natural product of their environment and the structure of the government that is their life, but they still have to agree with the point of view for it to create a binding enslavement.

Once an agreement has been made by the slave with his condition, then he only needs to learn to say, "If you don't tell me what to do, I fear to do anything." Remember, the fear of punishment is always operating in the mind of the slave, and most slaves would avoid risk-taking on new, self motivated assignments for fear it would be perceived as subversive or rebellious. If there is one trait a slave should not reveal to his master it would be pride. Pride would reveal self-direction and that is wholly unnecessary. Pride would also show self-awareness and self-appreciation which are unacceptable. Neither of these two traits are helpful to slave owners who need their slaves to simply *obey* without any thought to *self.*

The slave's need for direction reveals itself in two simple ways in their mindset. First, the slave heart may have tremendous trouble completing any project that is not clearly directed by another to its completion. After all, what is the reward for completing any project if there is no direct reward from the master of food or provision at the completion. The slave can be satisfied with only completing the portion of any work which grants him immediate and measurable reward.

Secondly, at first chance for freedom the slave heart may obsess over gaining a place in the ruling class in order to find new personal value. After all, the slave's mind only knows two systems: those who direct, and those who need direction. If he leaves the latter, then the only system left to engage is the former, the ruling class. This is why there is so much political heat and power struggle between "labor" and "management" even in modern times. These two categories of people view themselves as two completely different classes. This way of thinking is sorrowfully hung on a slavery system where the upper classes rule over the lower classes, and each one must fight for his position and value at all times. The tragedy of this system is that taking a place in any part of that system is dehumanizing. It is dehumanizing because it doesn't allow individuals to be intrinsically valuable as people, rather it requires them to kick, fight, and scratch out their place of security in this world.

This is why the slave-minded person, who when promoted out of the lower class into the ruling class, can become the most ruthless competitor in the arena of power and political authority. This might be exampled by slave-mentality rap artists who rise to money and power only to show how dehumanizing they can be as they rule both their former *masters* and their women and children with dehumanizing force. This might be exampled in the leadership style of labor union bosses who rise up out of the slave class (labor) themselves. They ruthlessly war against the corporate enemies of their collective souls and fight for every deserved payment the lower class demands to receive with a vicious sense of self-righteousness. In both cases the slave-minded person has moved classes in terms of outward position, but not internally in the perspective of the heart and it always shows.

Both of these revelations of how a slave may act, whether passively in retreat away from measurements or aggressively toward competing in class warfare, are both overcompensations— but in opposite directions. One is a compensation of passivity. One is a compensation of aggression. both are working to overcome the punishing affects of competition and judgement. Neither compensation will answer the heart's real question, "Am I fundamentally valuable because of who I am ... and not just because of what I do?" This is what we mean when we say that a slave lacks an intrinsic, personal value. Slaves are stuck with a more demeaning personal-worth formula that hinges on, "Tell me what to do so I can be valuable."

We have now seen that slavery involves struggles with *place, competition, punishment,* and *direction.* God has a heart to rescue both the natural and the spiritual slave. It is to God's rescue that we must now turn our attention and learn how a slave can not only be freed, but also be freed from the whole slavery system. We must learn how we, who have suffered under the mindset of slavery, can take on a whole new way of seeing ourselves and our eternal destiny!

THE PARABLE OF TWO SLAVE-SONS

It is time for us to turn our full attention now to how these general understandings of natural slave culture give us insights into the culture of the spiritual slave. There is a parable in Luke 15:11-32 that should be renamed the parable of *Two Boys Who Didn't Know How Much Daddy Loved Them.* It goes like this:

> There was a man who had two sons. The younger one said to his father, "Father, give me my share of the estate." So he [the father] divided his property between them. Not long after that, the younger son got together all he had, set off for a distant country and there squandered his wealth in wild living.

Here begins the sad tale of one son who had no idea how much his father loved him. He was the first of two brothers. One exemplifying a slave heart that shrunk back in passivity, and one that shot forward in aggression, both trying to deal with the struggles with their slave-spirit. The first son was passive. He did not see himself as his father saw him, and so he took his inheritance in the form of independence and tried to find his place in this world through self-fulfilling pleasure far away from the judgement of his father.

After he had spent everything, there was a severe famine in that whole country, and he began to be in need. So he went and hired himself out to a citizen of that country, who sent him to his fields to feed pigs. He longed to fill his stomach with the pods that the pigs were eating, but no one gave him anything.

We can see he thought of himself as a slave, not a son. He sold himself into slavery as soon as he had a need and no resources to meet it, and had no hope that anyone would have any reason to help him or to give him anything. He didn't go out and invest in himself or strike on in a new venture on his own, rather, he immediately asked others for direction and money. He had a slave heart.

When he came to his senses, he said, "How many of my father's hired men have food to spare, and here I am starving to death! I will set out and go back to my father and say to him: Father, I have sinned against heaven and against you. I am no longer worthy to be called your son; make me like one of your hired men." So he got up and went to his father.

This is how we know for a fact that he had no idea how much his father loved him. He had no idea that he was truly a son. Even as he plans to return to his home he only does so as a slave who will beg for a spot in the workforce. We have to ask ourselves, "How does a young man take his inheritance as a son from his father, leave home, and then immediately lose touch with any shred of his own identity as a son?" I believe the answer is in understanding that he *never* saw himself as a son in the first place. This young man never thought that sonship was true for him, and so when he left he simply had opportunity to prove it. No matter how this young man viewed himself in this parable there is no master-owner role who was going to agree with his slave mindset —there is only a father waiting for him. That fact didn't change the lost son's heart even when his father made it clear:

> But while he was still a long way off, his father saw him and was filled with compassion for him; he ran to his son, threw his arms around him and kissed him.

Of course the eyes of a father never change. The father could only see a son, no, *his son* coming down the road. No matter what his son has done, no matter where he has been or how he has failed, he will always be his son! But, sadly, this did not change the heart of the son.

> The son said to him, "Father, I have sinned against heaven and against you. I am no longer worthy to be called your son."

Even now the son who never really understood he was a favored son continues to negotiate toward slavery. He really believes he is a slave, but not even the son's desire to be seen as he saw himself—a slave—would change his father's point of view. The father exclaims with all his actions, "You are my son!" and refuses` to agree with the slave spirit in his own beloved son.

> But the father said to his servants, "Quick! Bring the best robe and put it on him. Put a ring on his finger and sandals on his feet. Bring the fattened calf and kill it. Let's have a

feast and celebrate. For this son of mine was dead and is alive again; he was lost and is found." So they began to celebrate.

We will give more attention to this beautiful moment a little later in this book, but for now let's notice how complete was the father's celebration of his son. He put on him his own robe, gave him the ring of authority, provided more food than he could eat, and called a public celebration to witness his favor and his love. The father defies his son's self-view and turns it on its head. This is what our Heavenly Father can do to our world, too, if we let him.

Then the story turns and we learn of another son in this father's heart:

Meanwhile, the older son was in the field.

Now, we are introduced to the second of the *Two Boys Who Didn't Know How Much Daddy Loved Them*. This one didn't try and satiate his heart's needs by running away and trying to find a life through lawlessness and sensuality. He didn't lower his head in acquiescence of the slave's position and wander off to live it out in shame. He did not go passive, on the contrary he aggressively pursued a place of noteworthy leadership in the father's work. He entered the competition. His was the compensation of aggression. He has stayed home and worked, and worked, and worked.

When he [this older son] came near the house, he heard music and dancing. So he called one of the servants and asked him what was going on. "Your brother has come," he replied, "and your father has killed the fattened calf because he has him back safe and sound." The older brother became angry and refused to go in.

Why was he angry? Simple. He had worked to establish his value in his father's eyes his whole life, and now in one moment all the honor and attention he had always wanted was being poured out on his brother the slacker. Tell me, dear reader, what son needs to work for his value in his father's eyes? Remember this young man didn't see this younger brother as a brother, no, he saw him as a competing slave, and he saw his father as the judging master. That's right. This older brother had also seen himself as a slave his whole life and had no internal clue that he was really a son. As a matter of fact when he looked at his own life's work he called it "slaving" and this self-look had fueled a kind of bubbling, undercurrent of anger in his life, his whole life, and now it was spilling out.

So his father went out and pleaded with him. But he answered his father, "Look! All these years I've been slaving for you and never disobeyed your orders. Yet you never gave me even a young goat so I could celebrate with my friends. But when this son of yours who has squandered your property with prostitutes comes home, you kill the fattened calf for him!"

There is no escape for the heart trapped by the spirit of slavery. Even when our own dear father is pleading with us all we can hear is the voice of a slave-master. All we can plead is how much we have worked, and how much we have earned by it. It is so important here to notice that the older son did not even imagine sharing a time of special celebration with his own father. He expected to celebrate out in a corner of the field with his own friends, but not with his father. No slave would celebrate with his master, that would be awkward and we can see the awkwardness in his own reply. A son's heart, however, is full of desire to celebrate with his father.

The father heart never agrees with the slave spirit in his sons. In this parable the father would not agree with the first son who had returned from his hiding, and he would not turn from this son who was shaking the angry fist of entitlement as a slave. In response to the shocking revelation of his son's enslavement to a lie against his very nature, the father, with love in his heart and hope that his son might understand, says all there is left to say:

"My son," the father said, "you are always with me, and everything I have is yours. But we had to celebrate and be glad, because this brother of yours was dead and is alive again; he was lost and is found."

I think this final note was to remind us of the foundational truth of the kingdom of God and how far both boys had misunderstood it: The Father loves his sons. Here the simplicity of the heart of a father is being expressed with no further need for argument or self-defense. He simply expresses his great love for what had been lost, his very own son. And when he says it so plainly the weight of a million revelations comes down on the cold, unfeeling, slavery-bound heart of his oldest son.

BEING SET FREE IS NOT ENOUGH

Those who are trapped in the mindset of a spiritual slave are, indeed, lost. They are lost from the care of their father. Every spiritual slave needs to return to his rightful place in the heart of God, who is our heavenly Father and would settle for no less than our agreement with him, "We are your favored sons!" Spiritual slaves are lost just like the spiritual orphan is lost and wandering the world looking for a place. The slave's search for value and the release from the crushing weight of judgement, comparison, punishment, competition, and grueling work only comes to an end with the Father saying:

"Son! Son, you are free!"

Here is the difficulty of the Gospel of Father's Love: we must agree with him in order to be free. This is the Gospel of the kingdom that Jesus preached and his disciples were trained to continue, namely, the Father calls you home and loves you with his whole heart ... will you agree?

Jesus said to those who struggled with the spirit of slavery (the professionally religious class), "If you hold to my teaching, you are really my disciples. Then you will know the truth, and the truth will set you free." He first said that we had to hold to his teaching. His teaching was not one of works, but it was one of our place in the Father's heart. Do you hold to your place of favor in the Father's heart? Then Jesus said that we would then "know" the truth and be free. He didn't say we would know about the truth. He didn't say that we would be privy to the facts. No, he said we must know the truth just as the *Two Boys Who Didn't Know How Much Daddy Loved Them* were always sons, but still they didn't know the truth. It was always true, it was all around them, but they didn't know it personally. Do you know the freedom of the Father's love?

The freedom of the Father's love is superior because it is not just freedom from something, but it is also freedom to something. Our freedom in Christ is more than a freedom out of enslavement. It is freedom into something we have always dreamed of. After all, it is not enough just to be set free and loosed, as it were, into a field of loneliness. Strangely, we get the idea from books and films that just to be free from bondage is enough. I propose, however, that a freed slave with no family, no father, and no sure provision in this world might be worse off than before. So it is with a spiritual slave who grasps for his freedom from enslavement to a system of working and competing only to find himself alone with no place in this world. Worse yet, he simply joins another slave system and another master because that is all he knows. We need to be freed into a new system. We need to be freed into the caring arms of God and the family of his love.

It is only when the call to enter the sure care and love of a providing eternal family is answered that the slave can truly be free.

WE ARE SET FREE INTO FAMILY

Jesus knew that being set free from slavery was not enough. This is why the Gospel is not good news unless forgiveness of sin and freedom from oppression are firmly connected to a call to join an eternal, real, loving family.

The kingdom he introduced is not a kingdom filled with masters and slaves. Nor is it, just as importantly, a kingdom of freed peoples who are unrelated and disconnected from one another. His kingdom is not a new enslavement where we are given doctrines and religious tradition so we can constantly divide ourselves and set our class roles accordingly. That would just be a new and improved slavery situation. Jesus proclaims a freedom into family who have a loving Father. He proclaims this family kingdom in Matthew 13:43 when he says of those who have eternal destiny with him, "the righteous will shine like the sun in the kingdom of their Father." It is a kingdom of family dreamed into existence by a Father.

Jesus enters this global problem of spiritual slavery with a global, eternal solution, which is exclusively: *family*. By accepting his invitation to family every spiritual slave can be free. He says in John 8:36, "So if the Son sets you free, you will be free indeed." Jesus promises a freedom that is truly complete and will be complete because a son, not an employee, inaugurates it.

It is a freedom, we must point out right at the front, that is useless for anyone who cannot admit or recognize that he is a slave. Look at what the Pharisees said to Jesus after he said, "If you hold to my teaching, you are really my disciples. Then you will know the truth, and the truth will set you free." These religious professionals who were in the top seats of Jewish culture and government, who had trained in the history and oral traditions of Judaism, who were well aware that the history of the Hebrew people had been completely filled with stories of capture and enslavement, first by the Egyptians, then the Syrians, then the Assyrians, then the Babylonians, and finally, the Romans who ruled the very ground on which they were standing and still they said in reply to Jesus, "We are Abraham's descendants and have never been slaves of anyone. How can you say that we shall be set free?" (John 8:33).

Unbelievable. They were blind to the truth because they denied the facts, and no one ignores the facts unless he his holding fast to another idea and therefore must ignore the facts in order to survive. We all, including the professionally religious men of Christ's day, must come face to face with the truth that the spirit of slavery rules in this world. When we do, the facts will have their way with us and we will wake up in a foreign land, bankrupt and lost. Have you admitted you have acted and lived like a slave, or do you flatly deny all influences of spiritual enslavement? Have you come into full view of your own history in the slave-system? Many have difficulty admitting their enslavement to the principles of judgement and competition especially after they have become big players in religious systems where those rules abound. We should not be surprised when many religious professionals scoff and walk away at our attempts to share the Good News of freedom in Christ. Sonship is a revelation that only the Holy Spirit can give, so we can't beat ourselves up if we are unable to convince a son of his true nature. Even the father in the parable of *Two Boys Who Didn't Know How Much Daddy Loved Them* seemed to be having an impossible time convincing even his own sons of their true nature. This is why sonship can't be guaranteed by attending a Christian conference or by reading this book. Sonship is the direct byproduct of the miracle of birth, and in our case, the miracle of a re-birth.

After these Jewish professionals blindly claimed to know nothing of slavery Jesus, in an attempt to rattle them, put it to them in such a way they could not deny, "I tell you the truth, everyone who sins is a slave to sin. Now a slave has no permanent place in the family, but a son belongs to it forever. So if the Son sets you free, you will be free indeed. I know you are Abraham's descendants. Yet you are ready to kill me, because you have no room for my word" (John 8:34-37). This is a moment of clarity like no other for those seeking to understand that the Good News of God is the Good News of Sonship.

A slave has no permanent place in the family.

Isn't this exactly what we have been saying about spiritual slaves?

But a son belongs to it forever.

This is exactly what we have said is the only answer to find true and lasting freedom from the burdens of orphanhood. Now we discover it is also the only answer for the crisis of spiritual enslavement. We must receive the adoption into the family as sons in order to overcome the spirit of slavery! It is the father's love that establishes our freedom. Our freedom is the freedom into sonship.

ADOPTION IS THE ANSWER

After Paul speaks for some time about the Law of God that was written on the hearts of humanity, and from which the rules of our enslavement are formed, he says in Romans 8:1, "Therefore, there is now no condemnation for those who are in Christ Jesus." Oh, what fantastic words to the heart of the slave who has lived in a constant state of judgement for poor performance and condemnation for failure! Then Paul continues to use the slavery picture to underline the fact that we have been freed from the old system of enslavement to judgement into the freedom of sonship. This is a new contract altogether and it is wholly different from the old system. The catalyst for the new formula is, as a matter of fact, the Holy Spirit who comes to convince us of our sonship. He says:

> Because those who are led by the Spirit of God are sons of God. For you did not receive a spirit that makes you a slave again to fear, but you received the Spirit of sonship. And by him we cry, "Abba, Father."
>
> The Spirit himself testifies with our spirit that we are God's children. Now if we are children, then we are heirs —heirs of God and co-heirs with Christ, if indeed we share in his sufferings in order that we may also share in his glory. (Romans 8:14-17)

That's right, it is from the Holy Spirit that we are given a new internal point of view. We are given the ability to cry out to God as our Father and receive our Father's love. I am so amazed at how thorough God has been in offering us a deep, complete solution to our need to be rescued from the spirit of slavery. He knew we would not only need to be set free, but that we would need to be able to receive a whole new system of understanding. We needed to be set free into a new kind of binding agreement, the binding covenant of family love. This is the new slavery that Paul speaks of in Romans 6:22, "But now that you have been set free from sin and have become slaves to God, the benefit you reap leads to holiness, and the result is eternal life." This new system is family and it is a kind of enslavement that is not filled with the atmosphere of punishment, but with the atmosphere of favor and joy as we serve our Father. In the natural we have no opportunity to choose when we are born into our family by a miracle of God's placement. However, we can choose to enter into our eternal spiritual family, and, amazingly, it will still be through the miracle of birth. We are born again into the Father's heart and forever contained in his love and favor. This is why Jesus tells Nicodemus who was a consummate slave-worker, ""I tell you the truth, no one can see the kingdom of God unless he is born again" (John 3:3). Birth is how sons come into the world. Slaves are bought, but sons are born. Our pathway into freedom is a new birth that comes by a miracle of Christ's life in us. We are all aching to experience this new birth, and the Bible even says the earth is aching as well:

> The creation waits in eager expectation for the sons of God to be revealed. For the creation was subjected to frustration, not by its own choice, but by the will of the one who subjected it, in hope that the creation itself will be liberated from its bondage to decay and brought into the glorious freedom of the children of God.
>
> We know that the whole creation has been groaning as in the pains of childbirth right up to the present time. Not only so, but we ourselves, who have the firstfruits of the Spirit, groan inwardly as we wait eagerly for our

adoption as sons, the redemption of our bodies. (Romans 8:19-23)

The earth does not ache to be recycled. The earth aches for the sons of God to be revealed so it can live out its true purpose—to be a nurturing atmosphere for the family of God. It is time for us to quit obsessing over saving our children from styrofoam cups if we haven't yet imparted to them their place in the family of God which takes care of much more systemic and far reaching poisons. Sonship heals the soul, sons heal the world.

So then, we cannot work our way out of slavery because that would be living out slavery's principles. This is also why so many try. The only way out of slavery is to receive a gift. Romans 6:23 says, "For the wages of sin is death [what we earn by our independent efforts], but the gift of God [what can only be received effortlessly] is eternal life in Christ Jesus our Lord." We must receive the gift of sonship from our heavenly Father. We can actually be born-again as Jesus told Nicodemus and therefore find ourselves with a new heavenly Dad ... and a new heavenly family.

IDENTIFYING THE DISCONNECT

Sonship doesn't just imply family, it demands it.

If a father adopts many sons, then the sons have no choice but to embrace one another as family. There are no sons who stand alone, the result of an isolated miracle. Our miracle results in an immediate corporate revelation. The Church is revealed to us in a moment. This is the essence of the Church Jesus is building: *adopted sons who embrace one another as family.*

How then can adopted sons who are embracing one another as family return to the old ways of slavery where there is competition, rank, judgement, and punishment? I submit it is just as Jesus said that we have not *known* the truth. Knowing the truth is so much different than looking at the truth from a distance. In much of our modern Church life we have learned to look at the truth of spiritual family from a distance.

Oh, we speak about the truth of spiritual family like it is a distant land yet unvisited—a land we love, nonetheless, but a land beyond our reach. When modern Christians talk about Church being God's family they do so with a list of internal disclaimers. We say it out of obligation but find few reasonable ways to really believe it. Church as family has become, for all practical purposes, a tongue-in-cheek saying. It has become subtle sarcasm. This is because we have tried to apply the word *family* on top of a system that is built on the foundations of slavery and it falls apart for us every time. It really is a believer's *inside joke*, but no one is laughing. Here are some of the ways we tell this joke:

- We call those who manage our organizations our *fathers* because that is all we know to do.

- We have called one hour teaching meetings *family time* even though we have no relationship with anyone sitting around us.

- We think of students in seminary as the *sons of our community* because the path of academia is the only path in our tradition that seems faintly like the journey of sonship, and then they arrive to rule us with the same management tools we unwittingly bought for them.

We have been putting a dress on a pig and it continually loses beauty contests. Why are we so disappointed?

Am I angry at the Church? No. Am I a raging cynic against all things everyday-Christian? No. Do I think school is bad? Of course not. What I am passionately against is the gross misappropriation we make with these terms: *family, Church, kingdom, community,* and *love.* I am simply saying that we are all familiar with these disappointments which roll into our lives when our terms for Christian life and the reality of our Christian life are harshly disconnected. What we haven't known how to do is express this disconnection without anger and cynicism. We haven't known how to express it without the guilty feelings of being disrespectful towards the only kind of Church-life we have ever been a part of. Cynicism is not a healthy response to a family in need, neither is hiding behind the door while your own family is being abused. We must learn to disapprove of this disconnection and bring health to the family without seeding a new war. What we need are loving voices and encouragements to help the spiritual slaves among us (and in us) wake up to the joys of sonship and to overcome the debilitating lies of orphanhood and slavery.

DECIDING TO MOVE ON

Remember, we fall into slavery when we choose to give power to the "laws" that we place ourselves under. Consider these; the laws of religion, the laws of christianity, and the laws of acceptable behavior. Webster's defines religion as a personal set or institutionalized system of religious attitudes, beliefs, and practices; a cause, principle, or system of beliefs held to with ardor and faith. So it's easy to identify religions like Hindu, Muslim, Christian, Jewish, Buddhist etc. But consider the observance of other laws that have created a religion of sorts ... like those who worship the earth and observe the laws of environmentalism or those who worship their philosophy and the laws of acceptable behavior. Those who are a part of any religion observe a list of laws ... the do's and don'ts of the belief system. Just like any other religion, keeping these laws creates a sense of OK-ness and the measuring tools to cast judgment at those who don't observe the laws. These laws tell us there is definitely a grid that we must adhere to in order to be in good standing at the heart level. The grid may contain social benchmarks like college degree, etiquette, popularity, conformity or non-conformity, physical attributes, fashion, style, and political affiliation. We judge one another by this acceptable behavior grid which is, more often than not, tied to our religious beliefs as well. This is the way of slaves, working for righteousness, and it will make us miserable.

We have to mature, and we have to overcome.

Little children are immature, and in many ways have to be told what to do just like slaves. Paul illustrates the idea that all little children are like slaves because in their immaturity they have to be told what to do by teachers and guides. "What I am saying is that as long as the heir is a child, he is no different from a slave, although he owns the whole estate. He is subject to guardians and trustees until the time set by his father" (Galatians 4:1). Paul is speaking of things in the natural as well as the spiritual. If a child inherits his father's estate it is put into a trust until he is old enough to manage it himself. That time is determined by the child's father who understands finance as well as the maturity of the child and his/her ability to handle the weight of the inheritance. This is seen in the spirit realm as well. Like in 1 Corinthians 3 where Paul addresses the Church of Corinth, "Brothers, I could not address you as spiritual but as worldly— mere infants in Christ. I gave you milk, not solid food, for you were not yet ready for it." Here Paul, as a fathering leader of the church, allowed for the fact that immature believers act like slaves when they are too young to understand that God really loves them as sons. We submit to you that all of Christian maturity is just learning to receive this word, believe this word, and act like ourselves ... to act like his sons!

Paul continues in his letter to the Corinthian believers: "Indeed, you are still not ready. So also we, when we were children, we were in slavery under the basic principles of the world. But when the time had fully come, God sent his Son, born of a woman, born under Law, to redeem those under Law, that we might receive the adoption as sons."

Wow!

Did you see that coming? [I assume you did given the trajectory of this book.]

He is speaking to our nature ... our beginnings. We were held in slavery to the basic principles of the world, and this means captured in the struggle of working for our love and right-ness. Christ was sent to us to actually buy us out of our slavery. He provides an escape from the "basic principles of the world" and the escape is a miraculous *adoption*. We no longer have to strive, we can immediately become part of the family. Now, we just have to believe it, and live in it. This is an amazing passage where we can see all of humanity as *the children of God*, but there is a critical transformation that takes place in us when we become the *sons of God through adoption*. It also says, clearly, that before we receive Christ we are definitely slaves, but even after we receive him we may still act like it for a while ... until we mature.

It is time to move on.

Continuing in Galatians; "Because you are sons, God sent the Spirit of his Son into our hearts, the Spirit who calls out, 'Abba, Father.' So you are *no longer a slave, but a son*; and since you are a son, God has made you *also an heir*." We must be transformed from children who live like slaves, to sons who understand their adoption and inheritance in God. Paul knew that immature believers could easily fall back into the old way of living like slaves ... but we don't have to. He says in Galatians 3, "Formerly, when you did not know God, you were slaves to those who by nature are not gods. But now that you know God—or rather are known by God—how is it that you are turning back to those weak and miserable principles? Do you wish to be enslaved by them all over again?"

What were these *weak and miserable principles?* These are the ways slaves can trade in knowledge, or trade in strength, or any other value system that might give them a sense of position in their spiritual social scene. These calendar events Paul noted were part of this slave value-trading as these believers tried to gain personal rightness by special rituals and calendar commitments. I know a lot of believers who do this every Sunday morning. These are temporary things we trusted in instead of trusting in Christ, which is to say, we were not confident that Christ had brought us back into the family of God via adoption, and so we continued working for a loving family just like slaves!

With that in mind let's take some time to look into what happens when believers trade in sonship and family and continue to believe and act like slaves. Here—elders, pastors, apostles, leaders—we have to make our own notes on how to improve our grace for the people of God. We have to search out new tools and new ways to nurture the people we love into their sonship.

CHRISTIAN SLAVES

When Paul wrote his letter to the Galatians he was writing to believers, not unbelievers. In this letter to troubled family Paul spends a great deal of time trying to persuade them to come out from under the lies of slavery and be who God had transformed them into being—sons. He appeals to them, "It is for freedom that Christ has set us free. Stand firm, then, and do not let yourselves be burdened again by a yoke of slavery" (Galatians 5:1). Yes, Christians can live like spiritual slaves. Paul knew it, and we must get a hold of it ourselves if we are to mature, and if we are to help others mature into sonship. The Christians in Galatia were really struggling in their maturity as sons. The spirit of slavery was not only influencing some of them, but it seems that it was being nurtured and cultivated.

CHRISTIAN SLAVES WORK FOR A PLACE

The Galatian believers were still working hard to gain respect in the eyes of those who would rule over them. They were receiving the directions of a ruling class. In spiritual culture people who rule over others are called by several names. One name that fits well is *witch*. A witch uses supernatural powers to achieve an outcome he desires. This usually involves using others to do so. This is why witches in classic literature cast spells on people in order to create the world they prefer and, likewise, in the Bible witches are those who cast controlling spells on others to get what they want. So, people who would rule over us with trickery and spiritual manipulation are witches, and witchcraft is the art of gaining control over others using spiritual tools. This is why Paul asks these slave-minded believers, "You foolish Galatians! Who has bewitched you?"

He knew there were master-managers at work among the Church in Galatia and he wanted desperately to see the people set free from their manipulations. Remember when he said, "Formerly, when you did not know God, you were slaves to those who by nature are not gods. But now that you know God—or rather are known by God—how is it that you are turning back to those weak and miserable principles? Do you wish to be enslaved by them all over again? You are observing special days and months and seasons and years! I fear for you, that somehow I have wasted my efforts on you" (Galatians 4:8-10). The intent of this passage is clear, and Paul's frustration is obvious, but I want to draw your attention now to one phrase that Paul inserts as a break in his thought when he is thinking of the Galatian's identity. He says in contrast to the idea that they knew God that it might be better to land on a lesser idea that they were *known by God*. Have you ever stopped to ask why Paul inserted this little disclaimer? It is just as we have said before, knowing about the truth is different than knowing *Truth* personally. Knowing about God is different than knowing God. You see, if the Galatian believers really knew God as their Father then they would be free just as Jesus has promised absolute freedom, but they were not free. Paul stuck in this disclaimer as a teaching jab: they were certainly known by God who loved them as his own sons, but they were living as slaves because they did not know and believe the father heart of God for them as sons.

Christian slaves will constantly be looking for things to do, and great missions to accomplish in order to prove that they are somebody in the kingdom of God. They can never be free from jumping from one task or one mission effort to the next. They never stop trading up to their next best doctrinal certainty or revelation to show they are on the cutting edge of Christian trends. Christian slaves are the most likely to jump on the next bandwagon that promises special provisions and insights into kingdom life. This includes the promises of Judaism-obsessed Christians who promise us a special place of favor if we keep Jewish festivals and ceremonies. It includes revelation obsessed Christians who obsess over websites that offer mysterious insights and prophetic revelations as a way to help believers achieve a greater place in the kingdom. It also covers tradition obsessed

Christians who cannot miss an opportunity to convince other believers why joining their kind of group would be an upgrade in their kingdom position.

All of these cultures offer what sons do not need.

Sons do not need to do anything to gain favor in the kingdom because they already live, by birth-right, as their Father's favorite sons. Can you tell when someone is struggling with knowing they are already Father's favorite son? This is a basic leadership discernment.

Christian slaves are also most likely to name drop the "Who's Who" whenever they enter a conversation about spiritual maturity, or if they have to answer a question that sounds like, "Who are you?" This includes dropping the name of the style of group, "I go to a house Church," or the denomination, "I am a Baptist," or the trendy website we have subscribed to, "Have you heard so-and-so's podcast? I think it is what's up." I am not saying that all of these references are inherently wrong, but I am pointing out that the words that lead a conversation usually are a window into the soul.

Slaves will be caught dropping the names of the leadership class they have chosen to align themselves with. I have a friend who can't have any conversation with me without dropping the name of a Christian writer, a controversial leadership figure, or a new personal mentor that has become the latest crucial influence in her life. It doesn't even matter if that figure is a Christian or not, because that is not the point. The point is that she has had trouble finding her own place in the world without someone else's position being established as the marker. Without the ability to tie a rope onto someone else's reputation or influence she could not understand where she was in the universe. This is a kind of leadership culture "work" that is designed to accomplish a "place" of security inside the fraternity of leadership. It is the work of aggressively associating with others in order to have a place next to them on the hill of accomplishments. Some of us have even gravitated to tying ourselves onto controversial, not-so-Christian influences, just because it immediately gives us notoriety in the sea of same-same Christian-culture-bots.

The only answer to this awkward need to work for a place on the hill of accomplishment is inside the rest of the Father's love and the rest that is offered to his favored sons.

Just this week I shared some time with some great men around a fire and good conversation. One of the men was new to our circle of friends, but he gave himself away as a man of the kingdom when he asked his first question of one of my close friends. He didn't ask him what he did. He didn't ask him about his associations. He asked, "Tell me about your wife and how you fell in love." Then later on he was asked about what his life adventure was like and he immediately broke into a story about his own kids and grandkids. Again, my heart rested in learning that this was a trustworthy man who was about the Father's business. Never mind that he was also a leader of an international ministry, has been in over 90 countries, and has worked alongside some of the great leaders of modern Christendom, this man has the heart of a son. Leaders, you too must commit to focusing on building family values even in the way you engage others in conversation. We can reinforce in one another the maladjusted mindset of comparisons and work obsessions or we can teach ourselves and others to focus on loving people, caring for our families, and being interested in one another's hearts. It truly is up to you.

CHRISTIAN SLAVES COMPETE

Of course slaves compete. How else could they know who was on top of the pile and worthy of more reward? How else would they be able to comfort themselves if they could not identify and look down on the losers?

This kind of competition in Christian slaves always leads to broken relationships and wounded communities. I say this because whenever the lens of seeing ourselves and others is through the looking glass of competition we can't help but treat each other as less than intrinsically valuable sons of God. Sure, we will treat some people with great respect, but only if they can promise us advancement in the game or if they can enhance our standing with others. Those who will get little respect are those who can offer us nothing and serve no utility for advancing in the competition. Those whom we offer disrespect will be those we consider obstacles to our advancement, or dead-weights on our ascent to higher levels. For the aggressive Christian slave other Christians are quickly reduced to little more than social utility.

I have found this to be most clearly demonstrated by people who get entrenched in missions or special ministry organizations without a clear view to the family kingdom of God. These environments, ironically, always espouse doing great things for others but create first a culture of doing great things in general. They promote helping the least of these, championing the poor, and rescuing the hurting. They promote praying for the nations, interceding for leaders, and they might fast on behalf of the whole world. The tragedy is that these same organizations turn out a regular production of tired, burnt out, relationally starved people who leave feeling, of all things, exploited. What? Why?

It is the culture of slaves to latch onto a great idea or a great job and to pursue it with all their might. It is in this very pursuit that a sense of worth is to be attained. Because of that very commitment, the commitment to the good, those who live under a slavery mindset are able to walk on the heads of their friends in order to accomplish the work they are fixated on. It is as if to say,

"We have a great job to do and regardless of the cost, including using you in complete disregard to your weaknesses, we are going to get it done." Ouch.

I remember a time in my journey that the spirit of slavery had me in its grip. I was on a summer missions trip with three other college students who were peers. We were to travel into the Pacific Northwest and share the Gospel with young people, especially, by leading week-long meetings in different fellowships from northern Idaho across into the Seattle area in Washington. The trip lasted for about 10 weeks. I think we were only in week one or two when Mitzi arrived to the chapel area where we were all preparing for an evening worship and teaching meeting, in tears. She sat down on the front row of the little fellowship covered in anguish. My other two teammates immediately went to her asking her what was wrong, and offering a touch of encouragement. They had no trouble pushing the pause button on the prep work to make time for her.

After a little bit she was able to articulate that her long time boyfriend had just broken up with her over the phone. She was devastated, was far away from home, and was surrounded by three people on this traveling team that she really didn't know. It was a lot to handle.

I never left the stage where I was tuning a guitar or looking over papers, I can't remember what trivial task I was performing, but I can remember that all I could think of was whether or not she was going to be able to sing that night and contribute to the leadership for that evening's meeting. She was the soloist who would sing a song or two in every meeting and all I could think were thoughts like: *Would she be able to sing? Would the meeting suffer if she couldn't pull it together? She is a basket case, I wonder if she knows how much more important what we are doing is?* Even as I type these words I feel a sweaty embarrassment about my insensitivity and calloused disregard for her feelings. I think I finally blurted out something stupid and hurtful that sounded like, "Well, I hope you can pull it together for this evening's meeting because we are really depending on you." I remember the looks I got from the other team members. At that time I didn't have enough sense to even be ashamed of myself.

Friends and partners in love with the people of God, we must repent for treating others so much like fuel for our machines. We must confess that we have often looked over the weak, and made demands of the strong just so we could accomplish what we thought was the great thing. There is more to the kingdom of God than just delivering messages and conducting meetings.

One of the ways, as leaders, we can begin to dissolve the atmosphere of competition in our fellowships and even in our cities is to begin to host more parties. That's right, parties. Christian leaders are so used to being called together under pressure to dream up great things to do, and to give reports on what great things they have been doing. In this mode they have learned how to avoid, deflect, and defend against more vision casting meetings or more leadership pow-wows. These kinds of meetings have become tiring and spiritually defeating because they imply more work for the slave-heart. This is why I say *throw more parties.* At parties we share food and fun. We laugh, tell stories, and watch each other act normal. Parties are where normal people learn how to be friends. It is time to be friends with your elders. Be friends with other pastors and leaders in town. Be friends with your team member and their friends, too. You will become a family man, and a very desirable friend if you only threw more parties and cancelled more meetings. If you are looking for a deeper meaning for such a silly sounding encouragement, then think on this from Romans 14:17, "For the kingdom of God is not a matter of eating and drinking, but of righteousness, peace and *joy* in the Holy Spirit." This Scripture teaches me that I can't reduce the kingdom down to just eating and having fun, but it might convince you that a lack of *joy* is one of the first signs of a fundamental lack of kingdom life. Go enjoy yourself and your friends!

CHRISTIAN SLAVES FEAR PUNISHMENT

How many of us have experienced a roller-coaster relationship with God where some days we feel up, up, up, and some days we are down in the dumps; and this cycle seems to be never ending? I have heard many people refer to it as their roller-coaster relationship with God. Growing up as a Southern Baptist we referred to it as "getting right with God" or "rededicating our lives." We did it every summer at youth camp and we had what we called a spiritual high. We might get one more *high* a year, if we rededicated our lives during a special Church meeting after a season of intense badness, some strong preaching on rock music, or the actual temperature of hell.

While the "highs" were pretty rare, the "lows" were usually long and deep and much easier to come by. Every time I sinned, thought of sinning, spent time with a sinner, or heard a sermon about a sin I was sure to feel bad. When I failed compliance with any number of Christian things to do I felt bad. The only solution I used to know was to try harder, do better, have a longer quite time, do more Scripture memory, go to Church more, and repent for my sins with more public drama. At one point, I remember vividly, my girlfriend was telling me how much she was enjoying her new Bible study and quiet time, and I, in classic slave competition mode, told her with a macho smugness that I was actually re-translating the whole Bible into my own words, longhand. When I think of that now I realize she must of thought I was a condescending, competitive, socially unaware jerk. That is, of course, because I was. The question now is, "Where did that drive to be such a jerk come from?" I think for me it was the drive to avoid the spiritual valleys. It was to avoid failure, and the guarantee of spiritual punishment that I would receive. My spiritual punishment was simply this: I would not feel close to God.

This was a punishing equation for my relationship with God. My heart's desire was to be near to God. I liked sensing his Presence and his love even at an early age. I loved the message of Christ's love and I almost always cried (and still do) when we read a Bible passage about Jesus miraculously healing a sick person. I loved Jesus as much as I knew how and then some. The pain entered in because I was absolutely convinced that the way he felt about me dramatically changed based on my actions. Good, consistent action was met with a sense of his Presence. Any bad actions were met with a sense of being isolated from God, like getting the cold shoulder from heaven. It was maddening and humiliating.

I had been bewitched and I didn't know it.

I had not been bewitched by mean people or malevolent leaders. No, quite the contrary, I was lead by wonderful people with a great desire to see me succeed in my relationship with God. The problem was the tools employed and the language used was a perfect fit for the broken information in my soul that sang the slave's song. Even the word *success* in the previous sentence implies that I could *fail* in my relationship with God. One book I refused to read even when all my over-achieving collegiate friends were carrying it around like a prize was a book called, *Many Aspire, Few Attain.* I don't want to know who wrote it (and my sincere apologies to the author), and I don't want to know what is in it (I never read a word of it so I speak out of ignorance of the true content), because from the title alone I believed if I read it I would never get out of the valley of my own failures ever again. I was sure I would find out that I was part of the "Many Who Aspired" and not part of the "Few Who Attained."

Looking back I would say that I was bewitched into my foolish failure fixation by a complex and well orchestrated demonic conspiracy. I believe the devil used and continues to use every tool, every voice, every book title, and every feeling we encounter to convince us that the slave's song is still *our* song. It is not our song. Ours is the song of sonship, yet we still hum the old tunes.

He uses religious people and religious systems the most because that is the garden in which most of us were planted when we gave our lives to Christ. These voices would have had no power, I must now remind myself, if I wasn't ready to agree with them. You see, these lying voices don't cease after we have becomes the sons of God. The enemy knows that he only needs us to believe what is not true about ourselves to cripple our journey into sonship. The enemy knows that even baseless lies still have power if we choose to believe them. Jesus made it clear that the truth would set us free. This clearly implies that we have to turn our back on lies. Once we realize there is no punishment for us inside of God's perfect love we can break the power of the lie that says *God loves you more when you are doing it right.* Once we see that there is no failure or success on our part that changes the speed of God's heartbeat of love for us then we can overcome the power of fear over our lives and walk in our sonship again. Overcoming slavery and orphanhood, in the most practical sense for the sons, is learning how to discern and overcome the lying voices in our own hearts, and then learning to sing the song of truth over ourselves.

One great series, teachers, you could commit to for ten weeks or more is the subject of the embracing, never-ending, overwheming *favor of God* which does not correlate with our failures or successes. Try it, and see what happens to the atmosphere of the place you serve.

CHRISTIAN SLAVES NEED DIRECTION

We have already written in the previous overview of the natural slave mindset that slaves need direction and that need reveals itself in two simple ways: First, the slave heart may have tremendous trouble completing any project that is not clearly directed by another to its completion. This is the passive approach. Remember, a slave is confronted with the fact that every moment in life is actually a Pass/Fail test. Every action and belief will be graded according to Success/Failure. So the slave heart sees the rule: *You must obey and follow the assignment to accomplish the good project for God* ... and then the slave waits. He waits because without a clear assignment his failure is almost certain. This is what many people call spiritual paralysis. It is the inability to move forward on anything in life with confidence unless pressed upon by a massive directional force. This directional force could be circumstances in life that force a decision. It could be the force of a strong leader, or the force of a very strong ministry organization's principles. The point to consider is that without the strong external force, the spiritual slave has trouble moving because the fear of failure is just too high. "I will wait until it is extremely clear," the slave says to himself, and along the way he discovers that this very passive approach to life always, always provides a way to blame someone or something else if his efforts then come to failure. Excellent [sarcasm]. If we always wait for clear external direction then we never have to be ultimately responsible for our own actions.

The second kind of response to the rule of accomplishing the great project for God is to ramp up into high control mode and blow all the other leadership voices off of the top of the hill of accomplishment. This is the aggressive response in the slave's heart. "I must outperform all other leadership voices, and prove that I am, indeed, in charge of this thing."

I have a friend who worked for Starbucks and exhibited these two conflicting responses, simultaneously, in his employment. It was he who, by the way, confessed to these competing, habitual responses and wanted help in understanding why he waffled from one to the other in cycles. On the one hand he loved espousing the idea that being part of a company that had clear rules and a clear method of order was a relief and a blessing to him. So, in many ways he could empty himself of all thoughtful responsibility at work and assume the passive, robotic position of doing everything by the book. On the other hand, he could not control his urge to tell everyone, including his manager, of how the book needed to be improved. This was the aggressive approach. He needed to show that he was actually smarter than all the rules of this impressive retail giant, and if no one was looking he had no trouble doing it his own way, which was the better way. The first approach got him quickly promoted, it was the second approach that finally got him fired.

I have another friend who has never seen a job, even in ministry, that wasn't too small to be impossible to finish. You read it right. It seemed that any job, no matter how small, could be put on the procrastination list forever. His responses to expectations, regardless of size was: "I will get to it, but right now it is too much for me. Why do they [people, society, life] want that from me? It is unfair." This was his passive response to the rules in his heart. By avoiding the personal responsibility to do the job he was also handily avoiding the responsibility to ever be graded for it. It worked great for him, but not great for the people around him who were constantly trying to rescue him from his own laziness. By the way, laziness is not the opposite of busyness. He was always too busy, but nothing every got done.

On the aggressive side, this person also had the ability to go "high control" in a snap and dominate a ministry project right down to the last detail proclaiming to others, "I expected more out of you," or "Now I have to finish it all by myself ... overnight." What a mess these last minute personal rescues created in his professional and personal life. This last minute, crunch time pressure is a perfect example of how a slave's heart can't move until it is forced to. In this example the last minute instinct to take over and fix a problem "the night before final exams" also provided the slave's heart the opportunity for excuses and denial of ultimate responsibility. It sounds like, "Well, you know I had to do that three week job in three days and so that is why it didn't turn out quite as good as I had hoped."

In summary, the Christian slave's heart needs external direction because the giving and following of direction is the basis of their sense of rightness in the universe. God never actually enters into this equation by rewarding or punishing the right and wrong actions on our list, but our conscience which is full of self-judgment is ready to do the job for him. Our heavenly Dad desperately wants us to break free from the cycle of needing external direction, so that we can enjoy the internal direction that he has given us. I believe with all my heart that God transforms our spiritual DNA code when he gives us our second birth into his kingdom. We carry his heart, his love, and his blood. All we need is to be free, then, to be ourselves. It is our destiny to enjoy the work of our hands without the constant over and under-compensations that fill up a slave's world.

We are to be free to enjoy our lives as sons.

Believers, take out a notebook and write down the answers to these questions on the pages:

- *What do you love?*

- *What are you great at?*

- *What do you do that is healthy and fun when no one is expecting anything from you?*

Ok, now wrap all that up into a short paragraph and try that on for a mission statement for a while. Call it: *The Mission To Be Myself.* See how much more your family smiles at you after a few weeks.

As a final note on the spiritual slave's need for direction let's take a look at the issue of rest. By affirming that slaves constantly need assignments we are also saying that the spiritual slave can never stop working. This means that the worst possible state in a Christian slave's life is the quiet pause in-between assignments. "Yack! Rest is for the lazy!" they say in the way they never slow down. Leaders, can you discern laziness from busy-ness?

Laziness, as you may know, is not the absence of being busy, it is the absence of productivity, so don't forget, spiritual slaves are often the people who are always busy, but never really doing anything. This affects our spiritual lives, our work lives, and our family lives. We have all heard stories about, or even lived into the story where, the parent was in the "ministry" and was never home, never available, and never attentive to their own children because of the great and mighty tasks of being involved in every aspect of traditional ministry work. It is intensely sad, and a crime against the family kingdom of God.

Spiritual slaves just can't rest. Why do you think some people struggle so much to simply obey the Commandment that simply says, "Six days you shall labor and do all your work, but the seventh day is a Sabbath to the LORD your God. On it you shall not do any work." The slave heart quietly yells, "Are you kidding?!" Slaves can't stop working, they will lose their place in line. Rest is at best an awkward difficulty and at worst an irrational myth in the life of the spiritual slave. Listen to the words in Hebrews "There remains, then, a Sabbath-rest for the people of God; for anyone who enters God's rest also rests from his own work, just as God did from his. Let us, therefore, make every effort to enter that rest, so that no one will fall by following their example of disobedience" (Hebrews 4:9-11). This passage is so direct for those of us who want to mature as sons. We must exhibit our sonship in our rest. "Their example of disobedience" was referring to the bloodline of Abraham who refused to cease their own slave-labor to earn a place with God and who refused to receive the Gospel of Jesus who came to give the rest of sonship—the rest of knowing that we have been given the gift of family and now we cannot earn it or lose it in our successes or failures.

CHRISTIAN SLAVE TRADERS

I want to speak directly to leadership now in order to draw attention to the ways we have brought the tools of enslavement to the people of God. It is time to confront these things and repent. We can change.

In Galatians 2:4 Paul confronted slavery instilling leadership methods when he said, "[This matter arose] because some false brothers had infiltrated our ranks to spy on the freedom we have in Christ Jesus and to make us slaves. We did not give in to them for a moment, so that the truth of the gospel might remain with you."

In 1 Corinthians 7:23 Paul says, "You were bought at a price; do not become slaves of men."

We are not to live as slaves when we are a free people, and we should, as leaders, do nothing that might encourage a slavery mindset. We are not to fall under the enslaving works of others, or in turn ever enslave those we have care of.

It was Abraham Lincoln who issued the Emancipation Proclamation that broke the power of slavery in the United States and led to the 13th, 14th, and 15th Amendments to the Constitution which further solidified the slaves freedom and the freed slaves' promotion to full citizenship with no legal class distinctions. Of course it took decades, and some would rightly argue, over a hundred years before this new citizenship really began to take place for black people in America. In some ways it is the fault of the oppressive work of the former slave-owner class who continued to inflict prejudicial thought and treatment towards all black people regardless of position. In other ways, however, it is because these former slaves took quite a while to believe the truth about themselves so they would be able to live into what the law and the constitution said was legally theirs to enjoy. The point I am making here is that just because someone announces that legally and factually you are free, even if Christ himself announces it like he did in John 8, you are not free until you believe it and walk in it.

Read this from Paul's letter to the Colossians 2:6-8:

> So then, just as you received Christ Jesus as Lord, continue to live in him, rooted and built up in him, strengthened in the faith as you were taught, and overflowing with thankfulness.

> See to it that no one takes you captive through hollow and deceptive philosophy, which depends on human tradition and the basic principles of this world rather than on Christ.

It is time for us to believe it and walk in it. Just as we received Christ as a gift, we now walk as sons because it, too, is a gift. We are free indeed.

Christian leaders, we have been prohibiting people in our care from walking in their freedom because of some foolish, repetitive actions and teachings. We might call this Christian slave trade because it supports the business of spiritual slavery. It is time to repent and change our ways. The next few sections will outline in more detail the ways we have participated in the slave trade and how we can start to abandon it.

SLAVERY IN MINISTRY WORK

Slave leaders constantly recruit. They recruit because there are positions to fill. There are positions to fill because there is a machine with well defined parts that must work together in order for it to run. Unless all the parts are in place and functioning then the whole machine will fall apart and the leaders won't get paid. If you have ever tried to manage that thing then you know the stresses. Some people have mistakenly called the job of running that "thing" *pastoring*, but of course that is just silly. Pastors love and nurture people, and managers run machines, but this is the primary stress of most traditional fellowship "pastors." They have a heart to do the first, but are required to do the latter in order to survive.

Bob called this the Spider's Web.

Bob Terrell is the man who first planted this understanding in my heart. He would quote the passage from Job 8:14-15 referring to the man who forgets God and his dependence on him, "What he trusts in is fragile; what he relies on is a spider's web. He leans on his web, but it gives way; he clings to it, but it does not hold." This idea of a man-made spider web is easy to see when men begin to manage the family of God instead of father them. The web represents the leader's design, the leader's *vision*. The things that get caught in the web will serve the spider's vision—that would be you and I. A spider weaves sticky words and sticky missions. It is easy to get caught, but it is much harder to get out. This arrangement is excellent if you are the spider. This is not great if you are the one caught in the web.

I warmed you up with this word picture so you would know that when I challenge you to abandon slave trading methods in your ministry work you won't think I am ignorant of the consequences. You will have to decide what price you are willing to pay. I am aware that if I ask you to stop weaving an enticing, sticky, attractive, visionary web then you are going to lose a lot of people, past and present, who would serve you.

I have a friend who sat with me a couple of years ago and said, in effect, "Ben, I can no longer keep the dog and pony show running. I just can't keep pushing all the buttons and doing what I have been doing to run the fellowship, and still call it *pastoring*. I am over it. What do I do now?"

He no longer wanted to rule the web.

He had taken a long sabbatical with his family and during that time he had come face to face with the increasing joy of sonship, and the diminishing reward of managing and leading according to his gifts of influence. He was tired, and even more importantly he was full of enthusiasm for what Church life could be like if the leaven of family was pressed into the bread of the fellowship. We took some time to discuss what that meant, and after a bit I told him the same thing I just told you: you will have to decide what price you are willing to pay. Things will change. Risk is scary for a reason, and people don't rock the boat for a reason. You have to decide what you really want, and what you are really willing to invest in the outcome.

He was ready to go all the way.

Here are a couple of the key things we repented of and set out to change right away:

First, he made a commitment to stop recruiting. He had to stop weaving new web. This was hard, but necessary. Most believers smell the motivations behind recruiting to roles and functions, and they don't want to have any part of it. It feels diminishing in many ways to be asked to fill a pre-defined role or function all on behalf of the great good—when there is little or no regard to that believer's own dreams, gifts, and personal sense of calling. The constant call from the stage to join this team, lead this ministry, or start this important new thing is translated as this to the ears of the hearers: *You are here to support my vision, and if you don't then the Church will fail.* What an awful trap.

Instead this leader decided to meet, along with the other key leader in the fellowship, with every single functioning family and member of the fellowship in order to discover what they dreamed about, what they wanted to do, and what they felt called to do. After that season of assessment he committed to allowing those insights into each believer to direct how they might be asked to serve or lead anything. In other words, if he found out that no one in the fellowship had a heart to start a youth ministry that, regardless of tradition or his own instincts, it was the wrong time to try and start one. This is how you begin to dismantle the web.

Secondly, he agreed to no longer grip the wheel of direction on everything the fellowship was doing. He had to move from the controlling center of the web where the spider has his discerning touch on every vibration of the people in his care. He had to release control over many areas of the fellowship's function whether it lived or died as a result. A practical move in that direction was to immediately remove the idea of "Senior Pastor" from the vocabulary surrounding him and the leadership team, and move to more Biblical language that included identifying *the elders* in the fellowship (of which he was one) and *the pastors* in the fellowship (who were not necessarily one and the same) and promoting them and commissioning them into leadership. This is how to kill the spider, first you starve the image in the mirror.

This move was slow and methodical, but also public. Leaders needed to be endorsed and publicly trusted, and then he had to make public commitments to give them the space to lead. This public endorsement and releasing is so important because it diminishes the slave-trader's ability to conduct back room deals to fix the machine and to apply emergency micro-management when things get shaky. Some people found this empowering and familial, some found it structurally threatening and relationally awkward.

Because this is a small book we can't go on discussing more of the things that this leader did in order to repent from leading from a manager's perspective and dismantling the spider's web, but we might push this one powerful truth: the Church belongs to Jesus, and he has commissioned no one to manage it. No one manages a family. One might manage the preparations for dinner, or the order in which the home is cleaned, or the schedule for recreation on the weekend, but no one can manage the actual members of the family in this way or we will lose the way of honor. We can nurture it, parents can lead it, we can give ourselves to the intimacies of relationship in it and wrap ourselves in its loving commitments, but we can't actually rule it or we will kill the very essence of it. So now we all begin our repentance by saying aloud:

• I repent for ever saying, "My Church" because the Church belongs to Jesus.

• I repent for treating others likes parts of a machine because the Church is not a machine and I am not a manager.

• I repent for believing that I have to give the people a vision or they will wander because we are not orphans, and we can all hear the Father's voice.

• I am committed to dismantling any web I have created so the people of God can live free as Christ has made them free.

SLAVERY IN DIVISIONS

Slave traders will always divide people. They have to because to a slave spirit the whole world is full of useful and unavoidable divisions: Us and Them. Saved and Lost. Mine and Yours. Pastor and Sheep. Protestant and Catholic. Clergy and Laity. Useful and Annoying. Recently, I think, the slave trade language has become more nuanced and sophisticated especially among younger fellowships and pioneering leaders. They like newer divisions like: Seeker and Satisfied. Emergent and Traditional. Corporatist or Small Church. Justice or Capitalist. I am not interested in discussing the merit or uselessness of any of these divisions. I am only interested in pointing out that leaders who have not settled into the joy of sonship and are still serving their slavery instincts simply cannot stop creating these new divisions. It is the language of advancement, separation, comparison, and identity. It is also the language of death because it destroys our very essence.

Would you consider repenting? I would encourage you to. I repent all the time. I still use some language that is divisive, but I have made a commitment to a lifetime of repentance because I do not have a heart that is divisive. I have the heart of a son. I have made a commitment to the Church who is only one even as I serve the Church who acts like a million separate parts. I believe that Jesus is not a polygamist and so I agree with him, and I will always disagree with teaching that creates more than One Bride, One Church, and One Family even if this creation is only in the atmospheres of our imagination. I will serve the Church as one even if she is divided in her own mind. Would you join me?

This commitment to repent from division and promote One Church does not lead to some sick, impotent universalism. That only happens to those who don't believe that God is always good so they lower the bar for him and everyone else as well. A commitment to One Family does not erase differences and promote homogeny, rather it refuses to allow differences to be the theme of our family reunions. When has the myriad disagreements between those you call your uncles, aunts, sisters, cousins, parents, etc. ever meant that you were any less a family? A commitment to One Family will allow us all to be just as different as we will be the same. Our commitment to One Bride will allow the beauty of every believer and every gathering to find a unique fit in our imagination so we can love her as Christ loves her. I know I want to respect the wife of Christ and honor her in every way. Would you join me?

Here are some practical ways to move forward in a very positive manner in breaking the power of slave trading divisions:

First, find ways to compliment the Bride at every occasion. Compliment those who are with you and those who are against you. Compliment the leaders of other fellowships in public and at dinner parties. Compliment believers and communities and their expressions and never end that sentence with, "but ... " for the devil whispers "but ... " in their ears everyday so there is no use in joining his song of diminishment.

Secondly, find ways to use the positive "we" when referring to the Church in your city. The Father loves his people in every place without preference or division and we have got to learn to do the same. It begins with our language. When you meet with your fellowship pray for the Church of the city, the people of God in your area, and bless all believers in your region with glowing language and positive terms. This is the leaven of family and if you press into the bread of your fellowship it can leaven the whole city.

One of the wonderful by-products of this attitude and language commitment is that it begins to remove the slavery mindset that traps people in comparisons even in an intensely local level. That is, even in your small fellowship the results of blessing the Church of the city will result in your group finding less division and comparison among themselves. The leaven of family togetherness really does rise in each of us and affect everyone around us if we choose to value it and promote it.

SLAVERY IN EVANGELISM

We must stop trying to persuade people to believe what we believe, and start inviting them to receive a family kingdom. The difference is not subtle and the outcome is not minor.

If we are trapped in spiritual slavery, and we are not free in our sonship, it will affect the way we love those who don't know Jesus. It works itself out in two distinct approaches as we receive the Great Commission which sends us into the world to make disciples who join a family kingdom. Watch what slave-believers will do ...

The first slavery approach to the Great Commission is born in the fear of offending our own conscience which continues to condemn us when we are living as slaves. The slave-believer focuses constantly on what is right and wrong according to knowledge and performance, because he is not at rest in his relationship with God. He gorges on the Tree of Knowledge of Good and Evil and refuses to enjoy the Tree of Life. If we fixate on what is right and wrong we will, by necessity, have to require everyone to immediately conform to all known laws of right behavior in order to *really be saved*. This slave-believer will spend a great deal of time making statements, writing blog posts, and joining traditions that diminish the value of those who do not follow Jesus or even practice Christian traditions the way they do. They must diminish other believers who don't teach the exact things they do. Folks, it is sad, but many have made their radio, TV, and local fellowship careers trafficking in the trade of slave values to other slave-believers who are trapped along with them. In the arena of loving unbelievers this is particularly pronounced. Take for instance my friend, Kay, who ministers to single mothers in the inner city. She does amazing work, loving these women and their children with Christ's love and giving them hope in their circumstance. She hosts Bible studies for them, coordinates projects between them and her local fellowship so that these women can make relationships outside of their environment, and works with them in many practical ways to rescue them from drug use, domestic violence and unhealthy lifestyles. She's led many to follow Christ and his beautiful family along the way and has seen some of them even begin to lead the Bible studies themselves. She told me of how some believers from her city challenged her that she "loved too much" and needed to share "more truth" with those women. I was quoting actual words there. These slave-believers were trying to sound benevolent, but we know what they really meant. These spiders were spinning a web and they wanted to catch Kay in it. They needed to fix these women up with more teaching and better doctrine so they would look more like them, talk more like them, coordinate with them, and not act so *unsaved*. This was prompted, of course, after they heard that some of these women use some profanity during their Bible studies, and from that flowed judgement against them because they don't know the righteousness that comes from sonship—only the false righteousness that comes from keeping the law. The seeds slave-believers sow are division, fear, judgement, and self-righteousness.

The second slavery-approach to the Great Commission is born in a fear of being rejected by the conscience of the world. This slavery, in other words, comes from the fear of man. Here is how the fear works itself out:

Slave-believers who are not free to be sons are also not free to really believe that God is always good. It is hard to enjoy the absolute sovereign goodness of God as a slave because sometimes he rewards, sometimes he punishes, and who can predict either? Slave-believers will find themselves being crushed under the weight of public opinion which is twisted against the goodness of God and the truth of the Gospel because of the slave spirit in the world. What happens is the slave-believer must constantly apologize for God and work to change the world's opinion of Christianity because without doing so they feel ugly in the eyes of the world. *God is not predictably good,* the slave thinks in the very back of his mind, *so I will have to cover for him.* Slaves always struggle with comparison and judgement no matter who is doing the comparing. It is a tough spot, because slave-believers love people and want to help them, but when they are judged by those same people for receiving and believing in Christ alone for salvation it puts a conflicting public pressure on them.

The slave-believer, without a mature sonship and the power of the Holy Spirit will often buckle under this pressure and choose to use the tools of slavery to fight back. Take for instance our friend Tommy who grew up in a city where Christians were mocked, rejected, and ridiculed professionally inside of the anti-Christian university culture. Tommy has spent most of his life into adulthood trying to ward off this constant barrage of diminishment, but some of his tools are slave tools. Tools of *comparison* and tools of *performance*. The comparison tool comes out when he preaches, "I am not like those other traditional Christians ... they don't really know God at all because they believe in hell ... and they don't recycle." (I am not kidding, nor am I making fun.) The slavery performance tools were applied when Tommy could no longer enjoy himself simply as a member of a beautiful family and needed to invent a new competition that he could come closer to winning. When these tools were applied in full force then he was became the leader and promoter of social activism to defeat capitalism and social injustice in order to prove God's goodness in the world. This was a kind of new, emerging competition among the hip and aware. The reason capitalism and injustice were connected in his mind, I think, had to do with America's reputation as a Christian nation and therefore Tommy needed to apologize for both Christianity and America at the same time. Tommy's self-punishment made everyone, including me, very tired.

Now, don't be offended at me. I did not say that calling for justice and resisting injustice was not a kingdom way of life. It is. What I said was that the slave-believer *must* do these things, and assume these responsibilities, in order to feel OK because he is *under the authority and judgment of a slavery mindset* while the son actually enacts justice naturally just by living and proclaiming the righteousness of Christ with every breath.

Kingdom sons do stand against injustice but they never, ever need to apologize for Dad. This is a defining difference between slaves and sons in social activism. One is making up for God's inactions, and one is trusting that everything God does is always, always good and perfect.

Kingdom sons are not afraid to ask God for healing, either. Slaves fear putting God on the spot. To ask him for something he might not do may cause him to ruin his reputation, and cause us to look like failures, too. *Better not to even ask God to heal ... at least without some pretty broad disclaimers like "if it be your will,"* thinks the slave to himself when confronted with sickness, death or the demonic. Sons ask anyway because the goodness of God is never in question, the healing heart of God is clearly known, and their reputation is nothing to be protected. Sons know their Heavenly Father is always good, no exceptions and this confidence grows from 1 Corinthians 2:14: "The man without the Spirit does not accept the things that come from the Spirit of God, for they are foolishness to him, and he cannot understand them, because they are spiritually discerned." This kind of discernment belongs to the sons, but constantly eludes the slaves.

SON

WHAT IS A SON?

In much of this book we have been defining sonship by illuminating what it is not. Sonship is neither orphanhood nor slavery. This is very clear. Along the way we have unearthed many of the basics of sonship by using the contrasting values of these other two world-views. Let's also stop here and affirm this foundational truth: *when we speak of spiritual sonship there is no gender.* Both men and women must receive their sonship.

In Galatians 3:26-29 we learn that: *"You are all sons of God through faith in Christ Jesus,* for all of you who were baptized into Christ have clothed yourselves with Christ. There is neither Jew nor Greek, slave nor free, *male nor female,* for you are all one in Christ Jesus. If you belong to Christ, then you are Abraham's seed, and heirs according to the promise." It is the miracle of the kingdom that brings us all together inside of his love.

I am a man. Yet, Christ has called me to be his bride. Is there a conflict? No. He is calling me to a place of love and commitment that in the natural only a woman can experience, but we are talking about spiritual things and, in Christ, we understand there are no gender divisions in the Father's heart for us. So, women, if I can be a bride, then you can be a son. When we speak of sonship we are speaking of the privilege and favor that we can understand in the natural and how that is transferred to all of us, regardless of gender or age or race, into the spiritual dimension of our relationship with the Father. Now, with that clear, it is time to head out on a new course where we can focus only on the heavenly, the positive, the promise of our destiny as sons. Let's begin by defining the joys of sonship in natural terms so we can understand the impact of sonship for all of us.

At the most basic and simplistic level a *son* is what we call a male child in relationship to his parents. The female gender synonym is, of course, daughter. These terms are so self-defining for us that using the term *son* to identify a male child is as exciting as calling water *wet*. As a matter of fact if you look in dictionaries for richer definitions you won't find any because this word, like the words *heaven* or *love*, have within them so much meaning that is simply not the work of dictionaries to try and handle them. We all know that heaven means more than the expanse above the clouds, and that love is more than affection toward another person, and now we will learn that sonship is eternally more meaningful than just being a male child. Let's look at some basic things we all know about sonship and that every culture in every time have known.

First, a son is the unique recipient of his father's essence. Whether we use biological terms like *DNA* or romantic terms like *heart* we know a son has them from his father. Even though both parents call their boy-child their son we don't classically say, "He's his mother's son!" No, we recognize that the son is carrying on his father's nature, his father's gender, and eventually he will grow up to take on his father's function as a father himself. For some reason God planted it in the human family that being a son held the unique expectation to carry out the purposes of the father. To expand our earlier point, when was the last time you heard someone say, "She's her mother's daughter!" Well, it's not because daughters don't have affection for their mother's ways, because they do, and its not because that bond is not beautiful or strong. It is because in the tradition of family there is an understanding that the father passes into the son his essence and that son is responsible to live up to the size and stature of his dad in some way or another. I have heard it said that a son should even go on and excel beyond his father, but even this statement firmly placed *dad* as the benchmark and solidifies the idea there is a unique transference from father to son unlike any other family relationship.

Let's pause here, again, and consider the role of gender in this discussion. Ladies, when I speak about sonship I am using masculine terms. I am not choosing to do so out of classic language usage or out of any prejudgement toward women. I am doing so in recognition of the fact that this is how it is Biblically expressed, and this is how we understand the uniqueness of the father-son bond and the transfer of heart and purpose. Of course mothers transfer great grace into the lives of their daughters but the expectation of that transfer has a different tone than the expectations of the son. Here are some basic things that we expect from sons that we don't expect from daughters, and I am, of course, generalizing to make a point:

Sons are expected to carry on the family name. When she marries, in most cultures, the wife takes her husband's name and she joins his family. It is not seen, generally, the other way around. There is a generational line drawn down through the ages, and it is drawn down the middle of the souls of fathers and sons.

Sons are expected to uphold the family's honor. This may sound Asian to the ears of English readers since we don't use this kind of language very much, but we all intrinsically know what this means. The honor of a family is the stature and reputation that is attached to their name. This family reputation will be known among their community and will be remembered through generations, and so sons are commissioned to act with integrity, fairness, courage, etc. because their actions reflect—like no other family member—on the character of the whole family. Because the family name passes down from father to sons, women are not classically admonished to uphold and steward the family's honor. (I realize this language is used in some cultures where men lord over their family like broken tyrants, especially the women, and use the word honor as an excuse to abuse and even kill those who offend their sense of reputation, but I think we can safely conclude that this use of the word is both perverted and of no good use. If anything its poor use by weak and evil men proves that the correct use of the meaning of the word is both good and useful.) I would like to propose that we consider the word *values* or *heart* when we think about the family's honor in our western mindset. It is the father's heart, the father's value system, that we expect to be transferred to all his children, and we expect them to carry on with their father's heart for things like integrity, honesty, hard work, respect for others, mercy, etc. This expectation, I believe, is most intensely expected from the first son.

Sons inherit their father's work, reputation, and wealth—regardless of the value of any of it. This transfer of responsibility and reputation between a father and a son is a two way street. The son may be expected to honor his father with his life and actions, but he will also be the recipient of his father's life and actions as well. Certainly, in modern times, the question of inheritance is no longer a limited proposal for the firstborn son, but we can still be sure the firstborn son will be keenly aware, more than any other family member, that the work of his father, the reputation of his father, and the wealth of his father have been laid on his shoulders and he will have to decide what to do with them. He can try and abandon it, or he can embrace it, but either way the son will have to deal with it, because these things are uniquely directed at him.

These three basic things that uniquely define sonship—name, honor, inheritance—are key ways we understand the usage of the word *sonship* now in our greater spiritual metaphor. We know that a daughter has a unique place in the father's heart, and he will relay that love and affection toward her in ways that are just for her. In that way daughterhood is unique only to the feminine gender. In the spirit, however, we understand sonship to be available to both genders. We know this because when we are encouraged in the Scripture to take on our role as brothers of Christ, and the sons of God, and to be heirs with Christ that we are being spoken to, all genders, all ages, all languages, all stations, equally. We are all called to sonship. This is where the passage in Galatians 3: 28, "There is neither Jew nor Greek, slave nor free, male nor female, for you are all one in Christ Jesus," really brings to light how God sees us and how we are to see ourselves.

So now, men and women, listen to these words because even though I am using masculine terms I am speaking in the spirit, not in a natural mindset. I am calling you all, ladies and gentlemen, to walk in your spiritual sonship. I am calling you all, boys and girls, to consider what it means to take on your heavenly father's name and pass it along to your sons in the spirit. I am asking you all, male and female, to consider what it means to know that you have daddy's heart, and you are expected to uphold the values he has handed down to you by the Holy Spirit. I am asking you, sons and daughters, to consider the fact that you are now expected to take up Father's work, to enjoy his reputation, and to share in his wealth that is your inheritance as sons of the kingdom. This sonship is real and it has given you a place that is firm and unchanging. Unlike the orphan who is never sure of his place, you are a son and you always know your place in the father's heart. You are carrying his name with you wherever you go, and you are never lost. This is your promise and your destiny, people of God, to walk on the firm ground of sonship so let's discover how to receive it more deeply and walk in it with confidence.

RECEIVING SONSHIP

We know our agreements with the basic principles of the world must end. Our slave-soul's need to work, work, work for absolution must end. Our wandering as lost orphans must come to an end. The only way to see the ending of these things is not in warring against them to defeat them head on, rather it is by turning our attention to the privilege and favor of sonship. Sonship will displace the other broken self-views with such powerful force that they shatter and scatter into the wake behind our new lives moving forward in Christ. The obvious challenge is that we will never accomplish our way into sonship, or achieve our way to daughterhood. We cannot satisfy a contract or form a more perfect community to gain ground with our Father. Sonship is truly a gift that only a father can give.

Well, then, what we are left with is terrifying.

In order to overcome the spirits of slavery and orphanhood we are going to have to receive a gift of pure, undeserved love from God. He is going to give us sonship, and we are going to have to humble ourselves and learn to receive it. He is going to visit our orphanage and pick us out, and we are just going to have to accept that this is really our day and we are really going to have a home ... and that we did nothing to make that happen.

Jesus came to prove that receiving and believing were, indeed our only hope. He came to introduce sonship in person, and then offered to share it with us. He invited us to be born again into his family, but first demonstrated in his own miraculous birth that we would have to follow him in like kind. We are to be born of both water and the spirit, both naturally and supernaturally.

When we receive Christ and believe in the miracle that he is for us, then there is nothing that can separate us from the lavish love of the Father because we have been born again as his sons. Romans 8 is a beautiful chapter on this subject and Romans 8:39 says that nothing "in all creation will be able to separate us from the love of God that is in Christ Jesus our Lord." Our proximity to God and our position in his heart is no longer in question when we receive Christ; what *is* in question is our ability to believe that the miracle is really true. We have tremendous problems simply living into what is true about us now that we are in Christ. The fact that the complete miracle of our new life in God is believing and receiving is really quite difficult for all of us. It would seem so much more natural if we could fight for it, earn it, or pay for the opportunity ... but we can't. All there is left for us in this grand exchange is to hold out our hands and receive. This work of humbly receiving can be so hard for us. We have been at the work of helping God out for so long it feels wrong to put down our tools, but we will never come into who we were meant to be as long as we continue to accommodate these lies that obligate us to earn his love. Jesus knew this would be the hardest part of "working out our salvation" (Phil 2:12) when he said "From the days of John the Baptist until now the kingdom of heaven suffers violence, and violent men take it by force" (Matt 11:12). The war we must wage is simple. We must war against any instinct that keeps us from receiving God's great, overwhelming, completely perfect love for us as a free gift.

While reading this book did you discover slavery and orphanhood in your own heart? Did you find places where you have left the safety of sonship to return to the elemental things that have soothed your soul in the past? Have you fallen into the trap of using self-measurements to give you the feeling of being *OK*. Do you sometimes entertain the basic principles of this world that tell you that you must work to win the love of your Father? I know I do. Well, these are simply the signs showing we all have difficulty walking in the reality of our sonship.

It is time to overcome what is nothing more than old habits.

Sonship is ours and has been since we received Christ. It is now time to walk in it.

It is time to make the truth of our sonship ring in the atmosphere around us. The first two sections of this book were unavoidably difficult for all of us. Whenever we have to illuminate our weaknesses and face our challenges we are going to suffer in it. Those two sections by necessity were filled with a lot of illumination of the *darkside*, and therefore they reminded us of where we do not want to go—what we do not want to be. This coming section to the end of the book is different.

From now on let's set our face on where we are going. Let's imagine who we want to be, indeed, who we really are at the core of our new beings.

What follows is extremely positive. So positive, as a matter of fact, that it may create a whole new kind of struggle in you. The struggle to receive amazing, expensive gifts can be crushing. What we are going to outline now are the beautiful, expensive gifts of God that you could have never earned, and you will only be able to receive them as gifts.

Relax. Drop your shoulders. Take a deep breath. There is nothing for you to do except hold out your hands. This is yours to receive.

RECEIVE THE LOVE OF CHRIST

In the book of Ephesians, Paul writes so powerfully and positively about the richness of the gift we have in Christ. He proclaims all the things we have received as a gift from God as a direct result of Christ's love for us. He sums up the partnership the Trinity has formed on our behalf when he says in the first chapter, verses 19 through 22:

> Consequently, you are no longer foreigners and aliens, but fellow citizens with God's people and

members of God's household, built on the foundation of the apostles and prophets, with Christ Jesus himself as the chief cornerstone. In him the whole building is joined together and rises to become a holy temple in the Lord. And in him you too are being built together to become a dwelling in which God lives by his Spirit.

You are God's Church, you are his building, and in you all together the Holy Spirit has come to live. All this is because of what Jesus has done for you out of love.

Verse 3 of the same chapter opens with "Praise be to the God and Father of our Lord Jesus Christ, who has blessed us in the heavenly realms with every spiritual blessing in Christ." He said *every spiritual blessing.* By receiving the love of Christ we can receive every spiritual blessing. Even as I type that sentence I am astounded by the truth of it. May God forgive me as I have often looked in every corner of my world to find the blessings that I wanted, but I have always had, available to me in Christ alone, *every spiritual blessing.*

I am stretching my hands out to receive every spiritual blessing from God through Christ's love. Without directly quoting each verse let me shower over you some of these blessings that we have in Christ, just by receiving him, and all of these can be easily seen in the first parts of Paul's letter to the Ephesians. I am going to paraphrase his words for all of us:

> God had chosen us from the beginning of all creation to be holy and blameless in Christ. In Christ we are holy. In Christ we are blameless.
>
> In his love he chose us before all creation to be adopted as his owns sons. This adoption comes through Christ alone, and it is our Father's great pleasure to

execute it. He set his heart on adopting us before the beginning of anything we know.

He has given us glorious grace. Grace is the energy for living and the power to excel in our true nature and it is a gift to us through Christ. The amount of grace he has given us is glorious and overwhelming. His grace for us is more than we need, too much for our requirements. We have this power in Christ alone because Father God loves him so much and has shared him with us and his love and grace explodes, now, in and through us.

In Christ, and by his blood, we have literally been bought away from the slaveholder and made to live as free men. We have been redeemed. At this moment he has forgiven us our sins, and has released us from every debt we owed him because Christ has paid it all. Christ's life was so valuable that when he gave it to us he paid more than the price required to cover our debt. His uncountable richness was poured out just for us and it was more than we needed.

God even gifted us with the ability to see and understand this beautiful mystery of his love through Christ. Christ himself is wisdom and Christ himself is understanding and now he is sharing himself in us. It was, according to God, his will and pleasure to give us this understanding in Christ just so we could enjoy how much he loves us.

In God's plan, through Christ who is sharing all this love with us and restoring us to his family, we are now God's own instruments of bringing healing and unity into the earth. God's people, the Hebrew nation and all the other nations who knew nothing about him, have now been brought back together as one people and it is exclusively happening in us as his newly adopted sons. We express Christ's unifying love as his *one body* in this world. It is his miraculous gift to us and through us.

I want to go on and on but I have only read to verse 10 so far. There is more and more and more! We would literally never finish this book if I tried to bring every blessing Christ has shared with us into print. After all, we have *every spiritual blessing* in Christ, so we may need many, many lifetimes to discover them all!

It is enough for us now to receive the ones that he brings to our attention. Believers, you must receive the blessings of Christ's love.

We pray aloud, "Jesus, thank you for blessing me with every spiritual blessing by sharing yourself with me. I want to receive you into my life. I want you to be my life. I choose to hold out my weak hands and receive the overwhelming gifts that are found in you alone. You are my God and my King, my savior and my friend, my grace and my power for everything called *life!*"

And now I am praying for you, dear reader, just as Paul prayed for the believers in Ephesus, and I believe he will answer my prayers in every way. I am paraphrasing Paul's own prayers as I pray for you:

> I am so thankful for you. Some of you I know, many more I do not, but I am thankful for all of you. You are God's own people, the saints of his Church. I am continually asking Father to fill you with the Spirit of wisdom and revelation that you could know him better. I pray for the Holy Spirit to make you smart in the truth of the kingdom, and of his eternal family. I ask the Holy Spirit to bring revelation to you in dreams, in prophecies, in the illumination of your mind and your imagination

so the things that are eternally true about Christ will be crystal clear to you now.

I pray also that the eyes of your heart, the seeing you do from your spirit, will come into a full view of the future you have in Christ. Christ is your hope and your future and I pray that you will come to see him and the amazing promise of eternal life in him as an intoxicating joy.

I pray that you come to know this: Christ has his own inheritance. He has his own treasure given to him by his Father. Do you know what it is? Or should I say, *Do you know who it is?* It is we, the saints. It is we, the Church, the apple of his eye, the prize flower in his garden, the ones for whom he died, and now we are the ones in whom he now lives. His power in us is transforming us into the beautiful, spotless bride that he is betrothed to marry for all eternity. We are his prize. We are his bride. We are Christ's inheritance. I pray that you will be crushed by the beautiful weight of this truth.

I pray that you will ride on the wave of his power. This is the same power God pressed into the earth like a mighty storm to pull his own son from death and then draw him up into the majestic realm of heaven to sit at his own right hand. This same power, I pray you will soon understand, saints, is drawing you up with the same death defying force to seat you alongside Christ in the same heavenly realm.

I pray for you, believers, to enjoy the non-negotiable fact that we sit with Christ far above all earthly powers and all earthly kingdoms. No power rules over us, no demonic force has reign over us, and no man can bring onto our heads any purpose because we are purposed for greatness in Christ alone. God has granted us this new perspective with Christ, from this great height, just so we can all get a bird's eye view on all the glorious gifts, the amazing grace, and the kindness in his heart toward us which he will display before us in all of creation and in every corner of both heavenly realms.

Holy Spirit, I am asking you on behalf of all the sons of God, to illuminate the depths of these things so that we can walk in them.

Amen.

In the book of Hebrews the writer explains our new position in Christ this way. 'In bringing many sons to glory, it was fitting that God, for whom and through whom everything exists, should make the author of their salvation perfect through suffering. Both the one who makes men holy and those who are made holy are of the same family. So Jesus is not ashamed to call them brothers. He says, 'I will declare your name to my brothers; in the presence of the congregation I will sing your praises.' And again, 'I will put my trust in him.' And again he says, 'Here am I, and the children God has given me'" (Hebrews 2: 10-13).

Jesus, himself, has stood in the court of the heavens and said about you, fellow believers, *these are mine, Father, these are the brothers you have given me. Here is your beautiful family, and I am proud to be among them.* You see, "Since the children have flesh and blood, he [Christ] too shared in their humanity so that by his death he might destroy him who holds the power of death—that is, the devil—and free those who all their lives were held in slavery by their fear of death" (Hebrews 2:14-15).

We have been set free from slavery and now we live as sons. We live as brothers of The Son. We share in his blessings. We receive from Christ, as we share this heavenly gift of sonship, *every spiritual blessing.*

Pause.

Receive him.

RECEIVE THE FATHER'S LOVE

Here it comes. Like a thundering avalanche down the mountainside just above you. Like the rush of the ground coming up to meet you when you dive out of an airplane. It is the width and depth of the Father's love. Inescapable.

Let's take these pictures of the uncontrollable largeness and power of the Father's love and convert them into a smaller visual that we can handle. Here is one. You are standing on the back of your father's '58 Chevrolet pickup truck. You are not standing in the bed where it is wide and safe, but you are up on the side rail of that bed where the edge is just wide enough for you feet and you are teetering just a bit. You are only four years old. Dad is standing down on the ground just a few feet off and he just turned to see you. In the surprise and instinct of the moment he just starts to lift his hands as you yell:

Catch me!

You know he will.

There was never a doubt, never a thought otherwise. As sure as the wind blows in your face the father's hands will rise to meet you. It is his heavenly instinct, his eternal joy, to catch you when you jump.

You jump because in his arms and in his grasp is always safety. The momentary perch on the side of the big blue step-side truck was much more frightening than the moment you spend in space on the way into your father's arms. Gravity? A mere concept. Physics? A meaningless word. What has meaning right now is the only sure reality in life as a trusting four year old: dad always catches me when I jump.

Come on, kids. Jump.

You see, friends, this kind of love is truly terrible. It has no regard for our performance, our self doubt, our unhealthy self talk, or our irrational rationalizations. It always catches us when we jump, regardless, and like a terrible avalanche it crushes us, but miraculously it rescues us at the same time. This love is the fire that both burns us and heals us.

This is why Jesus addressed those who were trying to trap him in the arguments and accusations of slaves and said of himself, and of his example of God's love, "Everyone who falls on that stone will be broken to pieces, but he on whom it falls will be crushed" (Luke 20:18).

The love of the Father must be received as a free gift. It has been his purposes all along to share his blessing with us. He has desired, according to Ephesians 3:15, to share his name with us so that we can join with him, with others here, and even with heavenly creation in enjoying the fact that we have a Father. We are no longer fatherless. We are his adopted sons, and as adopted sons we are his rightful heirs and we share in the reach of his arm, the rescue of his love, the sustaining power of his breath, and the sweetness of his kisses on our heads.

It is the nature of sons to cry out, "Daddy!" So friends lets cry out together:

> Daddy, God, we receive your love. We receive you as our Heavenly Dad. We are your sons, and we are the treasure of your heart. Thank you for sharing your son, Christ, in us so that we, too, could be your true sons. You are the source of our true DNA, the well of our very lives, and it is in your family that we have discovered our

true last name. We will become just like our heavenly Dad. We were created in your image, Papa, and now, in Christ we have the power to fulfill our destiny in you. We are proud of it.

This is not the ending place of our relationship with God, it is the beginning. When Jesus first teaches us to pray he says, *repeat after me,* "Our Father who is in heaven, Holy is your name ... " The word *our* was not a mistake. We join with Christ, and only by his free gift of love for us, can we use the word *our* and imagine Christ as our present company when we call out to Father God. God as *our Father* is the beginning and forever feature of our eternal relationship with him.

Let's remember the gifts the father gave his son when he returned to him in the parable of *Two Boys Who Didn't Know How Much Daddy Loved Them.* In Luke 15:22-23 the story's climactic moment sees the father running out to his returning son and "the father said to his servants, 'Quick! Bring the best robe and put it on him. Put a ring on his finger and sandals on his feet. Bring the fattened calf and kill it. Let's have a feast and celebrate."

The robe was a symbol of the father's identity.

The robe has long been a symbol of identity in many cultures and over many generations. A color, a sash, an embroidered pattern may all convey something about a person's identity. Slaves are not permitted to wear the family's robe of identity. A son is a member of the family. A son is entrusted with the identity of the family. The father called, immediately, I might point out with no cleansing ceremonies or public apologies required, and said, in essence, *Make sure everyone knows ... this one is my son.* This confidence is yours to share. The robe of his identity is a reminder to you, the world, and even the spiritual enemies of your soul that you belong to the Father's house and he will watch over you for his namesake!

The ring was a symbol of the father's authority.

The ring was a common ancient symbol of authority and of commitment to a family's purpose. A signet ring, as they were called, had engravings molded into them so that documents could be sealed with wax stamps to prove the authority of the one executing the document. Fathers passed along copies of their signet rings to their sons in order to empower them to do the work of the family, with the full authority of the family. Others were given copies of the original seal's mold so they could double check that any document claiming to carry the family's approval was, indeed, sealed with the correct ring. Even in the common Roman culture of Jesus' day fathers gave rings to their sons to mark their transition into adulthood and the sharing of responsibilities in the affairs of the family. Today, what we have left of this tradition we find in marriage where husbands and wives exchange rings as a way of saying, "What I have is yours." This is yours, believers, now to share. Your are to receive from the Father his ring which will give you authority to execute his business wherever you go. When the authorities of this world ask you where you are going or what you are doing you can answer, *Don't you know I have to be about my father's business?*

The sandals were a symbol of the father's trust.

Slaves were permitted to be barefoot, but sons were expected to wear shoes as a sign of their privilege. What is more, I believe, is that shoes signified the equipping of a son to go and to do the family's business both near and far. Isn't it amazing that the father gave to his wandering son—the son who had left him and broken his heart—*shoes*. He gave him shoes that he might leave again. You see, it's not that fathers don't ever want their sons to go and be who they are destined to be, they certainly do. What fathers want is for their sons to walk in the blessing of their family wherever they go. The younger son had taken his inheritance but did not go inside the father's blessing, but now he had returned in order to submit himself to the purposes of his father. Friends, it is time to put on the shoes of the father's trust in you. Papa trusts you to carry out his work wherever you go. There is no place in this world you can go that you won't walk in his blessing and in his trust.

The calf was a symbol of the father's excessive provision.

I have always laughed at the notion that he called for a whole calf! Seriously, he could have said, "Quick, make my boy a sandwich and break out the best wine." His son would have been satisfied with only a sandwich, and all the family would have needed to celebrate was some wine, but the father calls for a calf to be killed. Yes, killing a special animal for a feast was an announcement to the whole household and maybe to the neighbors and town as well that the son had come home. Certainly this said to the son's wounded heart, *I am proud of you and I want everyone to know how much I love you,* but I think there is something more. Remember, this young man had run out of food where he was and in his poverty he realized he could do better in his dad's house even as a servant. This repentance was humiliating for him. He returned with the thought that he would only ask his father for a sandwich and a corner of the servant's quarters to sleep in. But the father calls for an entire calf to be killed, and this shows the son, and it shows you and I, that the father's willingness to provide for our needs goes beyond what we could ever ask or dream for. He will waste his resources, as it were, on showering us with provision. Father wants to pour out his provision on you in abundance, not in breadcrumbs. It is time for you, sons of the kingdom, to begin to trust the father for what is yours as a son: wildly excessive, irrationally generous provision for your life.

RECEIVE THE HOLY SPIRIT

If we can't receive the power of the Holy Spirit, then we can't receive the power to act like sons. If we can't receive the counsel of the Holy Spirit, then we can't understand our new nature and how to be ourselves. If we can't be close friends with the Holy Spirit, then we refuse intimacy with the only member of the Trinity whose purpose is to be near us, teach us all things important, and help us in this world. In summary, if we refuse intimacy and friendship with the Holy Spirit we are destined to fall into the trap of slavery and orphanhood from sheer ignorance of our own sonship, and the powerlessness to act in accordance with our new, true nature as sons.

Paul says it like this, "Because you are sons, God sent the Spirit of his Son into our hearts, the Spirit who calls out, 'Abba, Father.' So you are no longer a slave, but a son; and since you are a son, God has made you also an heir" (Galatians 4:6). So let me ask it this way, What other gift has been given to you that will cry out from your once orphaned and slaved heart, "Abba, Father?" Will you be able to cry out like that on your own? Will you be able to cry out from the depth of your soul to your heavenly Father as a result of intense personal discipline and willpower? I believe, sadly, that many Christians over many generations have certainly tried. I tried for a long time, myself, and then I just gave up. I had to give up on my commitment to remaining comfortably protected from the Holy Spirit's power in my life because it was draining me of the resource I really needed. I wanted to overcome the spirit of slavery, but I was simultaneously afraid of the manifestation of the Holy Spirit in my life. As it turns out I had to repent of my judgments against him and I had to embrace the Holy Spirit as friend and partner. The Holy Spirit is the resource to cry out to Father God and overcome the spirit of slavery.

When I was growing up I learned to think of the Holy Spirit as an honored member of the Godhead that didn't do anything that we really needed anymore. I was taught to celebrate everything he had done in the past whether in miracles, revelation, healing or guidance, but I learned to be suspicious about anyone claiming to have received his work in the present. There were many reasons for this, actually, but the chief reason was nothing more than jealousy and judgement from the hearts of slaves. I remember the righteous, white hot anger that rose up in me when I heard someone even say the phrase, "God spoke to me." I was so angry and jealous that God would speak to them and not to me (I didn't think) that I wanted to shout, and sometimes did, "He doesn't speak out loud to anyone anymore!"

Now that we are receiving our sonship we have all been released from envy and jealousy. We have relaxed into the love of the father. In his acceptance we don't know any other instinct except to say *yes* to whatever he offers. He offers the Holy Spirit and we comfortably say, yes.

Try it. Say aloud, "Thank you Father for the Holy Spirit. He is a gift from your hand, sent by Jesus to minister to me, and I receive him in full. Fill me with the Holy Spirit, baptize me in his power and presence. All you have for me is what I want."

Developing a relationship with the third member of the Trinity is very important. After all he is the only member of the Godhead who is here with us right now. Yes, it's true. When Jesus taught us to pray where did he say the father was? That's right, *in heaven*. And where did Jesus go when he rose from the dead? That's right, *he ascended and now sits at the right hand of the Father.*

But where is the Holy Spirit? Jesus said that when he went away that he would send the Holy Spirit to be with us here. He said, "for he lives with you and will be in you" (John 14:17). The Holy Spirit is the God that we know and feel and encounter in this world.

Now, before you think I have put God into limited spaces as though he were limit-able be sure that I am only repeating to you what Jesus told us about himself and the assignments of the Godhead. Jesus taught us that his Father was in heaven, that he was going to go back to be with his Father, and that he was sending the Holy Spirit to us to be with us here. Make of it what you wish, but this is at least an encouragement to get acquainted with the Holy Spirit. Come on, the least we can do at this point is decide to become best friends with the Holy Spirit. Believers, it is time that we received the work of the Holy Spirit among us, honor his presence with us as the sovereign God, and recognize our need to walk in his power and presence.

He is ready for us, are you ready for him?

Let me encourage you again in the first ministry of the Holy Spirit: He is the fountain of our sonship. It is from the deep well of the Holy Spirit within us that we cry out *Daddy, Father* when we talk to God. He was given to bring proof into our hearts that we are truly sons.

In John 14 Jesus promised to send us a Counselor who would be with us forever.

Forever.

We need the Holy Spirit, you see, forever, not just for this life. We need his help and his grace for us. God has assigned himself as the Holy Spirit to integrate with us and counsel us forever. And what kind of counsel will he give? Well, the Scripture says in this passage that he will teach us all things and remind us of everything that Jesus has taught us. I am so amazed. This promise reminds me as a son of how I have *every spiritual blessing* in Christ, not just some blessings, and now here I find out that the Holy Spirit is actually going to *teach me all things* ... not just some things. I believe the first thing he teaches us, the first thing he reminds us of and then will continue to remind us of for all eternity is this: *You are the Father's son.*

Apparently God always wants us to exist and identify as his sons. Why do I say that? Well, in verse 18 Jesus says to us, "I will not leave you as orphans." So we see we have an eternal counselor who will teach us all things, but his sovereign purpose for entering our lives in the first place is to rescue us from orphanhood. I can imagine the Holy Spirit walking with each of you looking for the chance to lean into your ear and whisper, "Don't forget, you are his son." This he will do for all eternity.

The Holy Spirit's work in rescuing us from orphanhood is more than his teaching work. He is called the firstfruits of adoption. This means he is the first blooming of the reality we recognize as the spirit of sonship. Sonship blossoms in us as the direct result of the work of the Holy Spirit. The Scripture says in Romans 8:22-23, "We know that the whole creation has been groaning as in the pains of childbirth right up to the present time. Not only so, but we ourselves, who have the firstfruits of the Spirit, groan inwardly as we wait eagerly for our adoption as sons, the redemption of our bodies." This reveals that our adoption is fully inaugurated in the Holy Spirit but is not complete until we have new, transformed, adopted bodies in the next life. So the Holy Spirit is singing the song of sonship in us now, but it will only get louder and clearer as we step into eternity and are able to sing it with the totality of our fully redeemed lives! Yes!

I can't stop myself, I just have to quote from the first part of Romans 8 now [emphasis mine]:

And if the Spirit of him who raised Jesus from the dead is living in you, he who raised Christ from the dead will also give life to your mortal bodies through his Spirit, who lives in you.

Therefore, brothers, we have an obligation—but it is not to the sinful nature, to live according to it. For if you live according to the sinful nature, you will die; but if by the Spirit you put to death the misdeeds of the body, you will live, because *those who are led by the Spirit of God are sons of God.* For you *did not receive a spirit that makes you a slave again to fear,* but you received the *Spirit of sonship.* And by him we cry, "Abba, Father." *The Spirit himself testifies with our spirit* that we are God's children. Now if we are children, then *we are heirs*—heirs of God and co-heirs with Christ, if indeed we *share in his sufferings* in order that we may also *share in his glory.* (Romans 8:11-17)

We are the people who are led by the Spirit of God. We are divinely being directed and guided in this life. He is speaking within us, testifying inside of us from spirit to spirit, that we belong to God as sons. He is teaching us all things. He is showing us all truth. He is reminding us of who we are ...

So the challenge I have for you now is simple: *receive the baptism of the Holy Spirit.*

Cease from your judgments against him and against that phrase. Release the Holy Spirit from his offenses, and release yourself from being offended. Forgive God. Forgive yourself. Forgive anyone and everyone who has brought suspicion into your heart about the Holy Spirit and receive his baptism.

I realize that I am spending a good bit of time on this encouragement for you. I made the decision to not gloss over this subject on purpose. You see, I believe this challenge is absolutely essential for you and I will not allow the enemy to convince us that we can just negotiate out of receiving the gift of the Holy Spirit.

As a slave I could not receive.

As a son I can receive. I can receive the gift of the Holy Spirit.

Let me encourage you with the simple Scriptures that touch this subject.

In Acts 1:4-5, we learn that Jesus asked his disciples to get ready for a new kind of outpouring of the Holy Spirit. He said this during the miraculous 40 days that he walked with his disciples after the resurrection, reminding them again of what was most important: "On one occasion, while he was eating with them, he gave them this command: 'Do not leave Jerusalem, but wait for the gift my Father promised, which you have heard me speak about. For John baptized with water, but in a few days you will be baptized with the Holy Spirit.'"

These are the disciples he is talking to.

They are believers and have been for quite a while.

They have followed him for three years, witnessed his death and resurrection, engaged Christ in his after-death body for 40 days, and still Jesus tells them to wait for the baptism of the Holy Spirit. It was during this same 40 day period that he miraculously appeared to them, according to John 20:21 and said, "'Peace be with you! As the Father has sent me, I am sending you.' And with that he breathed on them and said, 'Receive the Holy Spirit.'" This command to receive was before they waited in the upper room.

Are these two Scriptures in conflict?

The answer is: *not unless your tradition has taught you that the Holy Spirit appears and reveals himself to you only once and all at once.*

Apparently, as we read so many different passages in the Bible, we discover we can receive the Holy Spirit, be filled with the Holy Spirit, be baptized with the Holy Spirit, be moved by the Holy Spirit, be descended upon by the Holy Spirit ... you get my point. The Holy Spirit is God. He can come any way he wants to, at any time he wants to, and in any measure he wants to. No matter how long we have known Christ, we can still wait on and ask for and expect the *increasing influence* of the Holy Spirit.

Acts 2:38   Peter replied, "Repent and be baptized, every one of you, in the name of Jesus Christ for the forgiveness of your sins. And you will receive the gift of the Holy Spirit." I love this Scripture because it reminds us that without calculating experiences, attending conferences, or speaking in tongues *we have all been promised the gift of the Holy Spirit* simply by receiving and believing in Jesus for the forgiveness of our sins.

Absolutely. It's a done deal.

Then later in the book of Acts we learn that the message of Christ is spreading everywhere and all kinds of people are receiving and believing in him. This means they were being adopted by God as sons, transformed into new life, and were receiving the gift of the Holy Spirit; however, here is an interesting moment that followed: "When the apostles in Jerusalem heard that Samaria had accepted the word of God, they sent Peter and John to them. When they arrived, they prayed for them that they might receive the Holy Spirit, *because the Holy Spirit had not yet come upon any of them;* they had simply been baptized into the name of the Lord Jesus. Then Peter and John placed their hands on them, and they received the Holy Spirit" Acts 8:14-17. Here we see quite plainly that the baptism of the Holy Spirit—the arrival of the Holy Spirit in power—is a definitive moment in the life of believers and was not the same as the promise of the Holy Spirit's presence when they first trusted Christ.

Are these two passages in conflict?

No, they are stating different things. Apparently, to receive the gift of the Holy Spirit and to receive the baptism of the Holy Spirit can be different things, and there seems to be no set rules on how that works.

Remember, early in Acts 2, just as Jesus had promised the disciples, "When the day of Pentecost came, they were all together in one place. Suddenly a sound like the blowing of a violent wind came from heaven and filled the whole house where they were sitting. They saw what seemed to be tongues of fire that separated and came to rest on each of them. All of them were filled with the Holy Spirit and began to speak in other tongues as the Spirit enabled them." This passage is why so many believers inseparably connect being baptized with the Holy Spirit and speaking in tongues. In Acts 8 Peter and John laid hands on the new believers and they were filled with the Holy Spirit, but it doesn't say they spoke in tongues. Well, they might have, they might not have, but somehow there was a manifestation of the Spirit, a tangible way for them to see and know these believers really had, "received the Holy Spirit." The point is they received the baptism of the Holy Spirit in power and it showed.

It was certainly not just the upper room disciples that received the baptism of the Holy Spirit and spoke in tongues. Remember, how God taught Peter that the good news was for both Jews and Gentiles? It was through the baptism of the Holy Spirit and speaking in tongues. In Acts 11:15-17 Peter relayed the story of how he encountered some Gentiles who were hungry for God, "As I began to speak, the Holy Spirit came on them as he had come on us at the beginning. Then I remembered what the Lord had said: 'John baptized with water, but you will be baptized with the Holy Spirit.' So if God gave them the same gift as he gave us, who believed in the Lord Jesus Christ, who was I to think that I could oppose God?" You see, here Peter wasn't even laying his hands on them as they had done in chapter 8, but still the Spirit came and baptized them while he was speaking to them, this time just like he had come in the upper room. These believers had the Spirit baptize them and, we assume because Peter said it was just like the upper room experience that the Holy Spirit descended like tongues of fire, or they spoke in tongues, or both. This convinced Peter without a shadow of a doubt that the good news of the kingdom was for all men.

Some of our traditions and fears have taught us that the baptism of the Holy Spirit will bring division. This is not true. The Scripture says in 1 Cor. 12:13, "For we were all baptized by one Spirit into one body—whether Jews or Greeks, slave or free—and we were all given the one Spirit to drink." The baptism of the Holy Spirit brings togetherness and one-ness. It is the mindset of slaves witnessing the baptism of the Holy Spirit that often brings division, not the mindset of sons who are being baptized in the Holy Spirit.

I realize that in this encouragement I have had to challenge our fears and traditions that might have hindered us in receiving this gift from the Father and that can be a tough work. I want to remind you that the promises for you as sons, through the Holy Spirit, look like this:

- You are to be eternally friends and hosts to the presence of God through the Holy Spirit. He will never leave you or forsake you. You will never be alone again.

- You are being reminded every day and every second that you are the sons of God. The Holy Spirit never ceases to work this into you. He is committed to seeing this truth come to life in you no matter what.

• The Holy Spirit is building you up with power. His power is otherworldly and it does not depend on you, your strengths, or your abilities. The Holy Spirit within you can and will do anything. You are now limitless in your ability to see and perform the purposes of God.

• The Holy Spirit is teaching you all things and showing you all truth. You are not destined to remain in the dark. You are sons of light, and as such you are to expect to understand everything about the kingdom of God. Wisdom and revelation are yours and you are to walk in them.

• Supernatural graces and abilities flow out of you naturally as you are baptized in the Holy Spirit. What used to be supernatural is now natural in you. You speak in tongues, you heal the sick, you see vision, you prophecy, you pastor and you give with kingdom generosity. You do all these things in obedience to the Father because you have Daddy's heart and you do the work of the Father as you are empowered by the Holy Spirit. Of course you do.

• You have banished judgement in fear as it relates to the work and expressions of the Holy Spirit in your life and the life of the whole Church. You are so aware of the Holy Spirit's desires that you expect him to manifest at every turn, in every place, in every way because he is eternally about his work with us here in the earth. You are a person expecting miracles, and a person of miracles. *You are a son.*

RECEIVE THE FAMILY

The sons' work is to be wrapped up in the family of God. This is what sonship requires. We are carriers of the family purposes of God. This is another way of saying that we are receiving and proclaiming the kingdom of God. You will notice here that I am not referring to the Church in the modern way we talk about *being involved in Church.* That is a wholly different matter. Being involved in gatherings, meetings and functions does not prove that the sons are wrapped up in their kingdom identity as one family in God. People are involved in Church life all over the world and a great many of them have still not embraced their sonship and have not received the good news of the kingdom of God. I am talking about how you, sons, are filled with the awareness that you are always representing the heart of God where you go, and you are always aware of your inclusion in his family no matter what group of believers or unbelievers you are with. This is the way a son walks around the world. You have been given the shoes from the Father which allow us to go out with our "feet fitted with the readiness that comes from the gospel of peace" (Ephesians 6:15). And so you are peacemakers on behalf of the family of God wherever you go.

It is the awareness of family representation and family identity that, for me, is a sign of someone's maturing in the things of the kingdom. I can tell by the way people speak of their ministry work, their fellowship, and their function in the world what they really believe, first, about themselves. I can tell, in other words, if you are walking as a son by the way you understand and express your relationship to the family of God.

I want to bless you to receive the family of God.

First, you must see the family. I pray for you now, "God, grant my friends eyes to see your family wherever they go. I pray the beauty of your family will be illuminated to them regardless of the place, the gathering, or the tradition, and they would be full of love and excitement for her."

In Romans 8 it says, "The Spirit himself testifies with our spirit that we are God's children. Now if we are children, then we are heirs ... " This is the promise of family lineage and family identity. Receive it. Say aloud, "The people of God are my people. I have people all over the world. I have family all over the world. I have brothers, sisters, aunts, uncles, sons, daughters, mothers and fathers in the spirit. I receive them all."

Paul goes on to affirm that it is the Holy Spirit in us that convinces us that we "who have the firstfruits of the Spirit, groan inwardly as we wait eagerly for our adoption as sons, the redemption of our bodies." To be filled with the Holy Spirit is a confirmation of being a child of God because it wells up in us to say, *"Abba, Father!"* and we know we are his and others are his as well. This stirs up a sense of belonging and a sense of love for one another. This is how we understand the words in 1 John 5 where the writer says, " 'Everyone who believes that Jesus is the Christ is born of God, and everyone who loves the father loves his child as well. This is how we know that we love the children of God: by loving God and carrying out his commands." Loving the children of God is within the commands of Scripture, but sons don't even need a commandment because it is their nature.

Once we see the people of God as our family, then we have to claim the ones close to us as our own. This is a call to name them one by one. To call out your relationships by name and say to them, using whatever words are necessary, *you are my family in God.* This is what sons do. They are proud of their family, and they know that preserving the family, honoring the family, and caring for the family are their top priorities. What is your top priority when you think about your spiritual work or your ministry calling? Well, I think it will become simply taking care of the portion of the family that we have the ability to touch. Those who don't take care of their portion will learn the lessons in the parable of stewardship in Matthew 25. Stewardship is taking care of treasure. God's treasure is people. For us to walk as wise servants watching over what God loves we must become sons who watch over the treasure of his family. This is your highest calling in this life.

It is important for us to receive, then, *the family* of God as a whole, and *our family* in specific. Sons will know to honor all their family heritage and all their family line stretching through generations and over oceans, but it will be to his family in his own household and in his own city that he will have to prove his practical commitment as a son.

Sons, you can stop raging against institutions and Christian organizations that have not been good to you. What did you expect from them? Jesus taught us to give Ceasar what is his and to give to God what is God's. I say to you, expect from men what belongs to men, and expect from the kingdom what belongs to the kingdom. We can't be disappointed when we squeeze a grape and out comes grape juice. If you squeeze the kingdom the wine of joy comes out ripe and mature. If we squeeze the organization of men then we will get out of it whatever they put into it—some of it great, some of it not so great. This allows us to repent from looking to the organizations of men, even the great institutions of the Church, to provide for us what only spiritual family can truly provide. You have ears to hear what I am speaking about. You can see and love the family of God both in and out of Church buildings. You can see and serve the family of God both in small and large settings. You can learn to identify your spiritual family one person at a time, which is the way family business is handled. You can love the Church global, but you can only receive the grace and responsibilities of family one person at at time. So:

- You can expect partnership from your brothers in Christ, but not from every believer that sits in a teaching meeting with you.

- You can expect parenting grace from your spiritual parents, but not from the leaders of your organization, per se.

- You can expect honor and respect from your spiritual children, but not from every young one you teach in a Bible study.

Do you see the difference between *your family*, and *the family*? You see, dear believers, we must release our hurts from those in *the family* that failed our expectations, because mostly we had wrong expectations of them as *our family*. It is mostly our fault that we were disappointed, and so we can take up the responsibility to forgive them. It has not helped us to take up continual offense at them, and to protest them. It is better for us as sons, and preservers of the one family of God, to forgive them all and release them to God.

RECEIVE THE FATHERS

Now we have come to an unavoidable part of maturing into the kingdom of God as sons. We know that we are to receive the Father's love. We know to receive the work of Christ and the Holy Spirit in us that places us into his family. We have even seen how, as sons, we are to identify and commit to our spiritual family. We are to call them by name and understand who they are to us like this.

Rita, you are my mother in Christ.

David, you are my brother in the Lord.

Gary, you are my son in the Lord.

It is now time for us to become comfortable, also, with saying *Doug, you are my father in Christ.*

If I were to speak this way to spiritual slaves they would pitch a fit. If I were to talk this way to orphans they will become confused and frustrated. When I speak this way to you who are maturing as sons, I believe you have ears to hear.

There are three kinds of earthly fathers for you to receive.

First, there is your natural father. Yes, believe it or not, sons of the kingdom must learn to reconcile with their natural fathers. This is an expression of being reconciled to Father God. Before you had a place in the heart of Father God you may have lost your way with your natural father. You may have placed many expectations on your earthly father that he could not fulfill because those expectations could only be placed on your perfect heavenly Father. Your earthly father was flawed and imperfect. Your requirements of him, in part, may not have been reasonable. Some were reasonable and he may have failed those as well. For both categories you now have the power to forgive. Before you knew your heavenly Father's love you could not have given grace to your natural father to be both great and weak, good and bad, because to do so would have threatened your own identity. This is why men who hate their fathers and proudly vow, "I will not be like my father," almost always repeat their father's sins. It is because you can't make a vow and break the identity that has been transferred to you by your natural father.

The only way to overcome the wounds and failures from your natural father is to face him directly, embrace him completely, and forgive him for his failures. You, sons, have the ability to completely forgive your natural fathers for their failures, and now in Christ you can bring honor to them and to your lineage and restore your place in your own family. This is receiving your natural father. It is not agreeing with him in everything, or approving of him in every way. It is saying, "I receive you as my father. I forgive you your failures, and I honor you for your grace toward me. I thank you for the gift of life in this world, and for the good in you that you passed on to me whether on purpose or accident it is no matter. Whether you failed or succeeded in your plans, I am your son."

Secondly, we must receive the fathers of the Church. This is such a rich admonition and I pray you will find joy the rest of your life celebrating the present and the past fathers in the Church. You see God has placed men to be fathers, and some in ways that bring great influence and foundations to the family of God. You have heard the phrase *early Church fathers*. The phrase exists because the Church, early on, had no trouble embracing the influence of men who served to father them into the things of the kingdom. It was a term of honor and endearment, and a way to express gratitude and respect for those who watched over them with the love of a father's heart. This is where Catholics still excel, and protestants fail miserably. Protestant traditions, in general, are so afraid of ascribing too much authority to men that might abuse it that they throw out the whole idea of receiving the fathers of the Church except in some antiquated and distant way.

Receiving the fathers of the Church means reconnecting with the fathers of the first century, and the fathers in every century after that. It is the practice of receiving the godly influence of fathering men in past generations and, in that way, restoring our sacred genealogy. I have heard it said that most modern Church leaders continually commit patricide—the killing of the fathers—in order to establish their own ministry, their own reign over the people of God without any reference to the fathers, the pastors, and the teachers that have come before them. This patricidal tendency robs us of the beauty of Matthew 1 and we skip over the genealogies found in the Bible as though they are just *pulp filler*. Genealogical lists are of extreme importance to God because they reveal his sovereign purpose *to accomplish everything through the family*. The only person in the whole Bible I know of who is specifically mentioned as having no genealogy was Melchizedek, Hebrews 7:3, "Without father or mother, without genealogy, without beginning of days or end of life, like the Son of God he remains a priest forever." Melchizedek was some kind of type or prophetic shadow of Christ who reflected Christ's eternal nature as our priest without beginning or end, but we still remember that Jesus' genealogy is promoted in Matthew 1 as a testament to the purposes of God to bring his own son into the world inside of the sacred line from Abraham through King David down to Christ.

So, now, if there were fathers in the early Church, why wouldn't there be fathers in the Church today? Surely, fathering love didn't go out of style in the 5th Century. No, of course not. We have to receive the fathers of the Church for today as well and honor them. I will propose to you a word now that is not used much in many modern traditions, but this lack of use is from the same origin as the lack of use of the idea of *Church fathers*. It is the word *apostle*. This word goes through the wringer, it seems, with every new generation or tradition trying to figure out how to apply it or how to avoid it. It has sometimes been the word institutionalists have used to give new levels of upgraded power to men in their flow charts of authority. Funny thing to me is that you never see the idea of *fathering* placed in a management flow chart of power. Fathers would not accept it.

We are called to receive our fathers in the Church today, and I believe it would be a great restoration of necessary grace if we could begin to understand them as apostles. I don't have any grid for understanding the teachers of mega-fellowships as apostles, or the leaders of pioneering mission organizations as apostles, unless ... unless they first show that they function first and foremost with fathering love and fathering hearts for the people of God. Paul made it clear to the Corinthian believers, "Even though you have ten thousand guardians in Christ, you do not have many fathers, for in Christ Jesus I became your father through the gospel" (1 Cor. 4:15). He was not their father because he taught them, or just because he first preached the Gospel there, or because he watched over them. To understand fatherhood in the spirit is just like fatherhood in the natural. He had adopted them into his heart, and they had received his fathering love. They had shared their identities with one another, and they recognized him as father, and he recognized them as his spiritual children. It was a love relationship given and received by permission. It was not an organizational position. In this way, sons of the kingdom, I ask you to look for and receive the fathers of the Church. You need more than guardians and teachers, or managers and leaders. You must receive the apostles. You must receive the fathers.

The third way we must learn to receive fathers in our lives is in receiving our spiritual fathers on a personal level. This encouragement can become the most tricky because we try and bring in our traditional understanding of leadership and government into it. We get confused because we try to make positions, we seek to fill offices, we start ranking and ordering folks into the qualified and unqualified. It all brings confusion, division, and jealousy with it. It is time for us to back up, take a deep breath, and as sons loved by our heavenly Father, recognize those who are, indeed, spiritual fathers in our journey.

Many of your spiritual fathers have come and gone and you never noticed or took time to say thanks. These men spoke words of life into you, put a hand on your shoulder and said *you can do it*, and reminded you of your favor in the eyes of God. They might have been on staff at a fellowship, they might have been a

Bible study leader, a camp counselor, a friend at work, or even your natural dad. At moments in time different people can offer the grace of fathering love for you and really be a spiritual father. Sometimes this is seasonal.

Many of you are looking around your sphere of relationships right now and you are saying, "I don't think I have a spiritual father." Well, relax, and don't let that sudden assessment drive you to anger towards me or anyone else. They might be there for you and you can't see them. After all, this is a pretty new challenge for you. They might not be there yet, because you have been living in such a way to repel those that might have fathering grace for you. Whatever the case, there is a recovery plan for you. Let's start with a simple prayer together, "Father, help me live and act more like a son. I want to be more attractive to spiritual fathers. I want to be humble, and teachable, and I want to be able to let others know that I need help. Father would you please bring spiritual fathers into my journey to love me and guide me into maturity as a son." I guarantee that prayer works. I dare you to keep praying it.

Some of you can recognize the eyes of someone who has watched over you with a caring, parental love for quite a long time. You can see the signs of his fathering love whether you have ever used those terms or not. It is time to celebrate his role in your life and to thank God for his placement in your journey, "Father, I thank you for the spiritual father in my life. I recognize all the seeds of the kingdom he has planted in my life. I commit from this day forward to honor him more with my words, my money, and my life as an expression of gratitude. I commit to letting him know how I really feel about him."

Again, it is not important to get hung up on categories, positions, seasons, or even titles. I don't have any need to be prejudiced toward spiritual mothers, either, I am just focusing here on the need for establishing the spiritually unique transfer between fathers and sons that we have outlined well at this point. If you like the words pastor, discipler, teacher, coach, then sobeit, enjoy those terms and celebrate those people for who they are to you in the kingdom of God. I am simply reminding you as sons that you are free to receive spiritual fathers. Before, when you thought as a slave, you could only receive managers. When you were orphans you could only receive guardians. Now that you are walking as sons you will find that it is easy to identify and enjoy your spiritual fathers.

HOW TO SPEAK LIKE A SON

Moving into the final pages of this book I only wish to give you some very basic practices for sonship. These are habits to adopt, tools to apply, and actions to copy that will allow your sonship to blossom. Don't mistake any one of these practices to define sonship because sonship is not a practice, it is state of being. Do look at each one as an action or an attitude that is natural for sons and, therefore, natural for you to practice and to become great at.

Let me show you some ways to practice sonship with your mouth.

I am my father's favorite son.

Now you say it.

I am my father's favorite son.

Isn't it true?

We know that fathers don't play favorites in terms of exalting one child over another, but I do know that as a father myself I can express this sentiment to each of my sons in order to show the favor I have for each of them. It does not invoke jealousy because I say it to each one with equal force and in front of one another. When they are together I tell them they are *both favorites.* You, son, are God's favorite. The best you can tell, when he looks at

154

you, there is no one else in the universe he could possibly love this much. So we practice saying things about ourselves that are true.

I have my father's heart.

Now you say it.

I have my father's heart.

Do we carry his DNA by the Spirit? Do we carry out his value system? 1 John 3:10 expresses this clearly when John says, "This is how we know who the children of God are and who the children of the devil are: Anyone who does not do what is right is not a child of God; nor is anyone who does not love his brother." The way we live and think proves whether or not we are God's children. I know I have the father's heart. So do you. Many will address Jesus as "Lord" as we enter the next life, according to the parable in Matthew 25, but because they did not carry out the heart of the Father on the earth they are not allowed to enter into his presence. In the natural this is plain to see as well. My sons literally have my DNA, and they are in one sense my children because of this basic biology, but that is not the same as me seeing one of them do something I love where I instinctively proclaim, "That's my boy!" The Father, looks on us as his sons and says to us by the Holy Spirit, "You are my beloved sons in whom I am very well pleased! That's my boy!" The Holy Spirit is reminding us right now that it is true.

This is our spiritual warfare. We are taking "captive every thought to make it obedient to Christ" not only in identifying those thoughts that speak slavery to us, but by seeding the atmospheres of our minds with the truth. I find the more I plant the truth in the air around me with my own words and my own proclamations the better I become at identifying lies, tearing down strongholds, and walking in the truth. We practice sonship with our mouths.

I will mention now some ways we practice sonship with our mouths on behalf of others. This is very important. Some travel a whole lifetime and never become excellent at blessing others with the treasured words that flow from sonship.

You have a destiny in God.

You practice saying it aloud while thinking about someone you love.

You have a destiny in God.

It is not natural for slaves to compliment and build others up, but it is now your nature as a son to do it always. Speaking to someone's destiny is a profound encouragement and a deep kingdom work. Reminding others that God has an eternal plan for them, and that you know they are headed toward it will remind them of their place in his heart. It will also remind them that they have a place in your heart. This is normal and natural because you have the father's heart. Everyone in this life needs to be reminded that regardless of the present trials and setbacks that God's purposes will come to life in them. It is a family purpose to see everyone released into their destiny in God. If you can be more specific about that destiny you see in others then feel free to share that too, but the important bottom line is that between them and God it is going to happen whatever it is.

You are a treasure to the family of God.

When you say it emphasize the word treasure. Say it aloud and practice.

You are a treasure to the family of God.

What an amazing compliment. Your confident sonship has released you to unload amazing compliments on the people of God. Reminding the saints that they are a treasure is a fantastic encouragement. It doesn't even require that you understand their gifts, or see them do anything great. I guarantee every believer you meet is a treasure for the family of God to discover. There is

Christ even in the least of these which means there is Christ to discover in every one. Jesus Christ is always our treasure, therefore every believer is a shining, golden treasure to be discovered, held up, and celebrated. You can do it, it is your nature to do it so practice often and on as many as you can.

There are myriads of ways to establish the family of God's identity around you. Everywhere we go we bless and call out our brothers and sisters in Christ. We make a special point to call out our fathers and mothers in the Lord and give them honor. We use our mouth to create the awareness of family all around us.

One other way I will mention here that we use our mouths to enact sonship is in worship. Worship is our opportunity to speak into the air the truth about God. We can worship with or without music, and even with our without words, but in this encouragement I want to call you up to vibrant, expressive, and verbal worship. I believe the sons of God are to be great at telling God how great he is. You, son, are to be great at expressing your heart of love to him. You are to lead in worship.

I love you Father. You are always good, and I worship you.

Try that aloud and add melody if you can.

I love you Father. You are always good, and I worship you.

We are a family of worshipers and we are filling the earth with his praises and outstanding tales of his greatness. "So what shall I do? I will pray with my spirit, but I will also pray with my mind; I will sing with my spirit, but I will also sing with my mind" (1 Cor. 14:15). This is a great way to understand how sons practice worship. They know in their spirits that something is true, but they are compelled to put it into their minds and their mouths therefore releasing the truth into the world. Music and worship songs are powerful ways to release the purposes and heart of God into our world. In Colossians we are told to, "Let the word of Christ dwell in you richly as you teach and admonish one another with all wisdom, and as you sing psalms, hymns and spiritual songs with gratitude in your hearts to God." Our grateful hearts will open up into songs that we share with one another. Sons, worship, and bring the truth of God's loving heart into the world around you!

HOW TO PRIORITIZE LIKE A SON

We know that sons have priorities that begin first with their own families. Natural sons have families to take care of. Spiritual sons have families to take care of. I might say the same thing this way: everyone has both natural and spiritual families to take care of. It would be nice if we could simply ascribe an exact formula for how that works, but I am afraid that I can't. I have learned along the way this is a complex algorithm that I don't quite know how to draw for you. For each person it will be different. For instance, a young married person with no children will prioritize their spouse first and then a descending priority list of spiritual and natural related family of friends, parents, siblings, partners, etc. in no guaranteed order. A married person in their sixties with both children and grandchildren, but none living at home, would still have their spouse first, and their own children, but they may also have lifelong friends and spiritual children that are so close to them that the lines blur for the prioritization of the relational tree. Many times it is a matter of prioritizing per issue, per need, and per season. The reason I bring this up is that Jesus, in two places I am aware of, gave us reason to understand that we do, indeed, have two families and we will need to learn to make priorities along the way.

> As they were walking along the road, a man said to him, "I will follow you wherever you go."

Jesus replied, "Foxes have holes and birds of the air have nests, but the Son of Man has no place to lay his head."

He said to another man, "Follow me."

But the man replied, "Lord, first let me go and bury my father."

Jesus said to him, "Let the dead bury their own dead, but you go and proclaim the kingdom of God." Still another said, "I will follow you, Lord; but first let me go back and say good-by to my family."

Jesus replied, "No one who puts his hand to the plow and looks back is fit for service in the kingdom of God." (Luke 9:57-62)

I believe this is a revelation about the priority of family for us all to consider. As we move through life we must prioritize those in our families, whether natural or spiritual or both, that need us the most. We prioritize those with whom we have the most necessary, intimate commitments during certain seasons. The seasons can change. Jesus knew when these people asked to follow him they were not willing to make changes in their priorities when confronted with responsibilities of taking on new relationships in the kingdom of God.

In Mark 3 there is another challenging moment for us to consider:

Then Jesus' mother and brothers arrived. Standing outside, they sent someone in to call him. A crowd was sitting around him, and they told him, "Your mother and brothers are outside looking for you."

"Who are my mother and my brothers?" he asked.

Then he looked at those seated in a circle around him and said, "Here are my mother and my brothers! Whoever does God's will is my brother and sister and mother." (Mark 3:31-35)

Jesus lived out perfect sonship for us. Even in this moment. It is difficult to see, but Jesus was showing us that we have two families. We have our family of origin, and our family of destiny. One you are born to, and one you choose. There will be times in life as we mature and go on with our callings as sons that our family of destiny will take priority. Our own natural families will have to learn of our great affection for the family of God and how much this family means to us. Sometimes, like Jesus, we will choose the spiritual family to prioritize in the moment. I do not believe he meant any disrespect to his mother, just like I would never want to disrespect my own mom, but we are still challenged here to consider our growing, morphing, changing family responsibilities.

There may not be an exacting rule for each detail, but we know this to be true no matter what: *family is always first.* Sons, it is time to put family first in all things. Family comes before work whether that work is in a coal mine or at a local Church. In either location the prioritization of our family, both spiritual and natural, is more important than the administrative, the entrepreneurial, the profitable, and the productive work we engage in. For the lead teacher at a local fellowship it means that some days your plan to study will be put aside by the needs of someone close to you in your family who needs to talk, but it might not warrant in interruption by a fellowship member that you don't know that well. What I am demonstrating is that your leadership office is not as important as your commitment to family, ever, and so your awareness of the concentric circles of relational commitment must always be in play. Those closer to the family center will always get your prioritized time and attention. This is just what sons do.

The second value in prioritizing our lives is in the Fourth Commandment: *Remember the Sabbath day by keeping it holy.* Holy means set apart for him. He commanded that we cease from basic labor, though Jesus taught us the commandment was bigger than a call to do nothing. He fed his disciples on the Sabbath and healed many people and when confronted by the lovers of the Law he explained that he was trying to teach them what the commandment was really about. Sons are free to enjoy the Sabbath day, he revealed, because sons are resting in the Father's provision. Slaves can never cease from their work. Slaves can't even rest when they are not working because the fear of not resting *in the right way* will torment their hearts. The Sabbath rest, then, belongs to the sons whose hearts are relaxed in the Father's love. Of course we can do good things and love others on the Sabbath, but we are commanded to keep it holy. Hebrews 3 and 4 explain that the true rest of the Sabbath day only belongs to the sons, because we have ceased from our labor in trying to earn our position with God. So the true Sabbath rest is this: *rejoice that you can relax and trust God for everything, spend a day considering how God is taking care of you.*

To keep anything holy we only need to keep it close to God. Remember, *holy* is a word that originates totally in God. It has no meaning apart from the God we discover in the Hebrew Bible . First, God is holy and he originates holiness. Other things that are holy either belong to him (are set apart for him), or are in close proximity to him. This is why bowls and utensils in the temple were called holy because they were close to him. It is how certain days or specific ground could be holy: because they were set apart for him, they belonged to him. It is also why we are commanded to, "Be holy for I am holy, " and then be identified as a holy priesthood and a holy nation already: "But you are a chosen people, a royal priesthood, a holy nation, a people belonging to God, that you may declare the praises of him who called you out of darkness into his wonderful light" (1 Peter 2:9). Amazing. We, through Christ, now fulfill both holiness requirements already, we both *belong to him* and *are near him* as well. This is how we understand that the Sabbath rest is natural for us as sons. We can rest from our labor, celebrate our relationship with God, and enjoy the call to rest with God as a family.

Sons prioritize family.

Sons rest.

Sons are excellent stewards.

Stewardship is a uniquely kingdom ability. Only sons can do it well. Those who do not walk as sons are also trying to steward, or take care of, or watch over their own resources and even the resources of others. Whether this is in their recent eco-fixations that challenge us to take care of the whole earth before it collapses, or in get-rich seminars where we are challenged to take care of our money so we can be rich, the themes of stewardship are traded and promoted at every turn. Everyone seems to be about the work of trying to take care of material resources so that they will, in turn, take care of us.

Strange concept, isn't it: the idea that *things will take care of us.* It is a neat idea, but is profoundly anti-kingdom.

We know that we have only one provider as sons and he is our Father. This is why only sons can be great stewards: Sons can remember where provision really comes from, and then, as a natural expression of their Father's heart, they can bring a joyful order to their world. This is our fulfillment of the commission in the garden of creation, to rule over the creation of the earth. Unbelievers and immature Christians will look to the earth for their provision, or look to the governments of nations for their care, but as sons we do not. As sons we look only to God and then in the authority he has given us we take care of what is ours to take care of.

Now, son, steward what you have watch over. Take care of your people and your city to the measure you have been given. Take care of your yard, your land, and your neighborhood as you can. It is not yours to rule another man's field or to tend other men's gardens, but to take care of your own and be an example for all to see. Bring order at your table, and bring order in your day. Establish order in your finances, and order in your investments. Look to no one but God for your provision, but work hard, and work well in order to earn a living and be a productive person. You honor your heavenly Father when you live out your courageous work ethic and believe in God's sure provision for you as you labor. Proclaim his provision for you and let no one mistake your prosperity as the guaranteed results of your labor. You do not lean on governments or entitlements, you do not trust in the arm of flesh. As a steward of your own resources you will not waste, you will preserve; you will store up some, invest some, and give a whole lot away.

Finally, as we encourage one another in our most important priorities as sons, we remember to take care of the poor and the helpless among us. We have the Father's heart and he invites the poor, the cripple, the lame and the lost to his parties. So do we. He visits the widows and the orphans. So do we. He preaches good news to the poor, binds up the brokenhearted, proclaims freedom for the captive, and visits the prisoner. So do we. It is for the least of these that we prove our Father's heart in us. To overlook the needy in our own towns, in our own neighborhoods is a kingdom crime.

We have two modern challenges to overcome as servants of the poor. First, it has become easier to defer the work of helping others because we have learned to trust institutions, governments, and programs to take care of almost every need among us, but it is not right for kingdom sons to live their lives without extending their hands and opening their lives on a personal level. The poverty you will encounter will be different in every place and in every season. Keep your hands open and your heart ready to give.

The second challenge we have is that we have often become confused between the call to cure poverty and to take care of the poor. The difference is enormous. To cure poverty is an incredible dream whose potential accomplishment I cannot speak to. I don't know how men would go about fixing the brokenness in all of humanity that leads to systemic poverty across the whole globe. I might be able to help on a micro level in my own town. But taking care of the poor is well within my grasp. It is in my nature to gravitate toward the poor and needy, and I enjoy challenging myself and my family to excel in it. I encourage you sons, rather than obsess over starting a new charitable organization to save an entire continent it might be best to learn how to become more accessible to the actual needy within a mile of your home.

G.K. Chesterton put it better than I will here since I will only paraphrase: If you really want to become actively engaged in the needs of others it would be better to think extremely local than to think globally at all. To think globally creates distance and generalization when what we need is the annoying proximity and the specific smells and problems of human beings with names. It would be much better, said Chesterton, if the *local* climbed down our chimneys and sat in our favorite armchair. This would do more to put us in touch with the real needs of humanity and the real trouble we have in helping them than any grand global plan. I only bring this to you here to encourage you. Everyone can help someone, but almost no one can help everyone, so do what you can for those God brings to you and trust the rest of the world to him.

HOW TO DREAM LIKE A SON

I have only a few short paragraphs left in me to finish this book. I want to speak to your divine imagination. By that I mean I want to speak to the dreaming and hoping part of you that transcends your natural mind and thinks about the possibilities in this life and in the life to come. These possibilities are neither rational nor expected. I have never thought that the sons of God should be that rational, after all, rationality belongs to the minds of men and our heavenly Father is not limited by our finite brain-power at all. It certainly is not rational that he continue to pursue us after generations of defiance and avoidance, yet he does with no less energy than he did with the first generation he placed on the earth. This leads me to conclude that our own attempts to help others do not need to be all that rational either. It is not rational to fall in love, but the best stories in all of time are on just the irrational act of passion and something called love that we have yet to put in a test tube and divide into parts. Sons should be given permission to dream wild thoughts about loving others and rescuing the hurting. They should be permitted to dream irrational dreams of redemptive works, and healing enterprise. And, I believe, specifically, that we should commit to dreaming irrationally about the size and scope of our inheritance as sons. That's right, our inheritance. We know we have one. We are joint-heirs with Christ.

Dream on sons.

What could this inheritance be? How much of it is there? Do we share in Christ's own sense of his inheritance in us? Is it eternally reciprocal? Will it come all in the future or can I enjoy some of it now? If so, what is it? What can we claim? These questions are not the greedy questions of slaves, or the improper grasping of orphans, no, this is the adventure of a son discovering the generosity of his dad's heart. I know that I revel in bringing new adventures to my own sons. I love to buy things for them, take them to places they have never been, and invite them to do scary adventurous things with me when their mother is not watching. What scary adventurous things is the Father calling you into? What is he trying to give you just for his own pleasure in seeing the look on your face? What place is he wanting to take you to that will unfold his purposes in your journey like you could have never imagined? As high and wide as you can try to imagine right now, you will not even come close to seeing the distant edges of his inheritance for you no matter how high you might scale to look.

It is time, dear sons, to believe in your unique call. There is no one else here on this earth with the same destiny in God. You are one of a kind. Your fields to tend are unlike anyone else's. Only you can take up your father's work in the place he has called you to do it. This is the mysterious stuff of fingerprints and snowflakes where there are so many of us, but not any two of us are just alike. Revel in it. Take pride in it. You are one of a kind, and God has seen to it that you have adventures to go on that will be known deeply only by you and the Holy Spirit. Whatever he whispers in your ear, do it. You've got one life here so make it a helluva ride.

At this point why even consider the fences and boundaries of this world? What is it about the limitations that men are constantly erecting around you that make them so powerful? What could possibly have enough power to hold you back from your destiny in God? Do you really need to wait, after all, for

God to open a *door?* You know what I am talking about. I hear Christians speaking of God opening and closing doors all the time. They speak like powerless stage players who would stand still in a hallway for the rest of their lives if God didn't reach down and grab the knob and turn it for them. You can live like that if you want to, or you might consider you destiny as a son. You might see a wall between you and your sense of calling in God and this wall might be three miles high and made of steel. Well, in my imagination I see you asking God for the most awesome diesel powered, steel cutting, super-chainsaw the earth has ever seen. You fire it up, and with a wink to the folks staring at their doorknobs you cut a massive hole in the wall that is blocking you. Sparks and shards of metal are flying all over the heavens. I can hear you yelling over the sound of the fierce engine, "Dad told me I was going over there ... God help me, that's where I am going!"

Now, sons, it is time to walk in your authority. When Paul speaks of the earth groaning and aching for change he is speaking to us. He is speaking about the sons of God. Romans 8:19 says, "The creation waits in eager expectation for the sons of God to be revealed."

Sons, reveal yourselves to the earth! It is so happy to see you!

I believe that everywhere I step the earth and all creation around breathes a sigh of relief and begins to relax. I believe that order emanates from the kingdom authority that I have been given and everywhere I go this order begins to align the very molecules of space. You think I am kidding? I am not. Sons, your very presence in the world is redemptive and healing. You have been given authority and commission to do even greater things than Christ did in his walk here, and so it is time you begin to expect it everywhere—and I mean everywhere—you go. All of creation has only one real purpose and that is to be an excellent place for me to dwell. That's right, all of creation was made for me, not me for it. When I arrive in creation anywhere God's purposes are closer to being fulfilled than ever before. Before I got there creation was looking for me like a puppy waiting for its master. The spiritual realm is waiting for you now to enact your authority as you pray, "Your kingdom come on earth as it is in heaven!" Yes! Pray it sons, and pray it believing. People can be reconciled! Wounds can be healed! Failures can be overcome and destiny can be restored! Kingdom order can be established and the family of God can dwell together in power and in peace in the places where you walk!

How can we walk in the authority he has given us to tread even on the heads of scorpions and over all the power of the enemy as Jesus promised us in Luke 10:19 if we don't choose, right now, to believe we have it. It will be too late if we have to cry out to God to give us authority after we have already stepped barefoot onto the scorpion won't it? It will be too late if we wait until the devil is coming through the window as the enemy of our family's welfare to put in a request for temporary authority don't you think? Sons, you must know what Christ has granted you authority in and you must walk in it.

Finally, do everything you do with the joy that God is watching you. There is no need to hide and no need to fear. His perfect love has cast out all fear because there are no more thoughts of failure and punishment. There is only joy and adventure in front of him. When you do pause to look toward the Father, as you are enjoying the adventure of your life, you will see that smile again. Every time you look there is that beaming, radiant smile that says, every time, but in a million different ways with joy and approval and pride only a father could know:

My son.

www.benpasley.com

CPSIA information can be obtained at www.ICGtesting.com
Printed in the USA
238392LV00004B/1/P